in_focus

MW01155106

Growing better
Cities

in_focus

IDRC's *In_Focus* Collection tackles current and pressing issues in sustainable international development. Each publication distills IDRC's research experience with an eye to drawing out important lessons, observations, and recommendations for decision-makers and policy analysts. Each also serves as a focal point for an IDRC Web site that probes more deeply into the issue, and is constructed to serve the differing information needs of IDRC's various readers. A full list of *In_Focus* Web sites may be found at **www.idrc.ca/ in_focus**. Each *In_Focus* book may be browsed and ordered online at **www.idrc.ca/books**.

IDRC welcomes any feedback on this publication. Please direct your comments to The Publisher at **pub@idrc.ca**.

in_focus

Growing better
Cities

URBAN AGRICULTURE FOR
SUSTAINABLE DEVELOPMENT

by Luc J.A. Mougeot

INTERNATIONAL DEVELOPMENT RESEARCH CENTRE
Ottawa • Cairo • Dakar • Montevideo • Nairobi • New Delhi • Singapore

Published by the International Development Research Centre
PO Box 8500, Ottawa, ON, Canada K1G 3H9
www.idrc.ca / info@idrc.ca

© International Development Research Centre 2006

Library and Archives Canada Cataloguing in Publication

Mougeot, Luc J.A
Growing better cities : urban agriculture for sustainable development / by
Luc Mougeot.

(In focus)
ISBN 1-55250-226-0

1. Urban agriculture — Developing countries. 2. Sustainable
development — Developing countries. I. International Development
Research Centre (Canada). II. Title. III. Title: Urban agriculture for
sustainable development. IV. Series: In focus (International Development
Research Centre (Canada))

S494.5.U72M68 2006   338.1'09172'4091732   C2006-980018-9

IDRC Books endeavours to produce environmentally friendly publications.
All paper used is recycled as well as recyclable. All inks and coatings are
vegetable-based products.

This publication may be read online at **www.idrc.ca/books**, and serves as
the focal point for an IDRC thematic Web site on urban agriculture:
www.idrc.ca/in_focus_cities.

Contents

1. The Issue ➤ **1**

In the past two decades, some enlightened municipalities have recognized the value of urban food self-reliance and begun to work with "urban farmers" rather than against them. Today, urban agriculture is increasingly on the international agenda, recognized as part of a comprehensive solution to the problems of runaway growth of cities in developing countries.

2. The Approach ➤ **13**

IDRC's approach to urban agriculture has matured into a well-orchestrated strategy: human expertise, financial resources, and institutional networks work in tandem to tackle gaps in knowledge or capacity that stand in the way of urban agriculture's contribution to healthier, more prosperous, equitable, and sustainable cities.

3. Experiences from the Field ➤ **25**

This brief review of some of the urban agriculture projects supported by IDRC offers a cross-section of the major issues confronting urban agriculture in Latin America, the Caribbean, Africa, and the Middle East, with the emphasis on policy-based research.

4. Learning from Experience ➤ **49**

Urban agriculture is not the total solution to the issues facing the future of cities in developing countries, but it is an essential part of any program to make those cities more liveable, and to improve the lives of city dwellers. This section offers practical lessons for city planners, politicians, policymakers, and urban farmers.

5. Recommendations ➤ **61**

More than 20 years ago, IDRC became the first international agency to formally support research on urban agriculture (UA). Many important lessons have emerged from that pioneering experience, lessons that are encapsulated in a series of recommendations for cities attempting to work with urban agriculture rather than against it.

6. A City of the Future ➤ **71**

Let's look ahead 20 years. We are going to take a tour of an imaginary city to see what the city of the future might look like — a city that has benefited from research, from shared knowledge, and has learned from the experience of other cities as well as from its own policy attempts to integrate UA and its practitioners in urban development.

Appendix 1. Glossary of Terms and Acronyms ➤ **79**

Appendix 2. Sources and Resources ➤ **85**

The Publisher ➤ **99**

Foreword

Paul Taylor
Director, Brussels Liaison Office
UN-HABITAT

The UN system's interest in urban agriculture began to grow in the early 1980s. This was about the time that a survey in Uganda by UNICEF and Save the Children concluded that urban agriculture (UA) supplied sufficient food and that there was no need for supplementary feeding programs, despite ongoing civil dislocation at the time. The steady rise of urban agriculture on the international development agenda over the next 25 years paralleled a rising involvement in many parts of the UN system, often in collaboration with pioneering research being supported by Canada's International Development Research Centre (IDRC).

There are many examples of this collaboration. Here are but a few:

- → IDRC supported several large surveys of UA in sub-Saharan Africa throughout the 1980s. The UN Development Programme made generous use of this early UA research in the seminal 1996 book, *Urban Agriculture: Food, Jobs and Sustainable Cities.*

- → The 1996 edition of FAO's *The State of Food and Agriculture* report, released at the World Summit on Food Security in Rome, included a section devoted to urban agriculture, drawing extensively on research from IDRC and the UN University.

- → In 1999, FAO passed a resolution calling for the coordination of its programing on peri-urban agriculture. IDRC was invited by FAO to the session that would adopt this resolution and made a plenary intervention in support of it.

- → In 2000, FAO, IDRC, and UN-HABITAT brought together mayors from Latin America and the Caribbean in Quito, Ecuador, for an international workshop to strengthen food security and participatory municipal governance. This event and its outcomes are featured in this book.

- → In 2001, during a special session of the UN General Assembly, FAO, UN-HABITAT, and IDRC organized a parallel event: "Food for the Cities: Urbanization, Food Security, and Urban Management."

- → In 2002 — at a workshop convened by UN-HABITAT, FAO, IDRC, the International Network of Resource Centres on Urban Agriculture and Food Security (RUAF), and CGIAR's Urban Harvest — government delegates reviewed world experience with credit and investment programs for urban agriculture. The lessons from this event were subsequently shared with delegates at the 2004 Second World Urban Forum in Barcelona.

Over the years, IDRC has both influenced and responded swiftly to the UN's evolving agenda, and it has done so as much through research and training grounded in local realities and local needs for technology and policy interventions, as through a systematic and effective dissemination of its work. In particular, IDRC has been associated with much, if not most of UN-HABITAT's programing for urban agriculture, it has supported FAO in developing and consolidating its own programing on the topic, and it has worked with both UN–HABITAT and FAO in joint exchanges, policy events, and publications on urban agriculture. Through its partnerships, IDRC has supported the design, testing, and packaging of a wide range of tools that international resource centres, regional research networks, and focal points of expertise are beginning to share with a larger audience.

Publication of this book could not be more timely. It reflects on IDRC's 20-year experience in a wide variety of urban settings in the developing world and draws from this experience a series of valuable principles that will help city governments to integrate urban agriculture into their strategies to meet the Millennium Development Goals. And it will help them do so in ways that will be comprehensive and flexible, inclusive and effective.

I commend IDRC for encapsulating and sharing so much in this short and readable book, and the thematic Web site that accompanies it. I strongly recommend both, primarily to municipal and national policymakers, but also to others with an interest in making our cities more inclusive, viable, and sustainable.

Preface

Luc J.A. Mougeot
Senior Program Specialist
International Development Research Centre

This little book distills two decades of research and development in urban agriculture (UA) and related issues by IDRC and its partners. Its publication, in conjunction with the Third World Urban Forum (WUF) in Vancouver, Canada, is particularly timely. It was in Vancouver, 30 years ago, that the first United Nations Conference on Human Settlements was held. That 1976 conference led the UN to create its Centre for Human Settlements — now called UN-HABITAT — an agency that is widely referenced for its work with IDRC in these pages.

One striking conclusion from developments in UA policy over the last 30 years is that, contrary to common perception, UA is neither the short-lived remnant of a rural culture nor a nasty symptom of arrested urban development. The real paradox is that, on the political agenda, UA is far more advanced in Northern countries than it is in the South — even where its practice would be comparatively less critical to the wellbeing of city dwellers.

In cities of the North, public UA initiatives initially promoted household and community gardening for food security in times of economic crisis (for example, the British Allotments Act of 1925 and the War Gardens of Canada, 1924–1947). Today, cities such as Amsterdam, London, Stockholm, Berlin, and St Petersburg in Europe, or New York, Philadelphia, Cleveland, Montreal, Toronto, and Vancouver in North America have connected UA with resource recycling and conservation, therapy and recreation, education and safe food provision, community development, green architecture, and open space management.

➤ Montreal has incorporated UA as a permanent land use of municipal parks; it has the largest community garden program in Canada, now managed at the borough level.

➤ Lisbon's pedagogical gardens, promoted city wide in the 1990s, led the city to develop a city farm, now visited by more than 100 000 people every year.

➤ Delft, in the Netherlands, has combined UA with several other land uses in a heavily populated polder area.

➤ In Parisian suburbia, inclusive local land development and management now protects cultivated landscapes for their nonagricultural services, which are highly valued by the public and various urban actors.

➤ Vancouver has created its Food Policy Council, which allows the city to integrate and coordinate the activities of its various departments in UA and other aspects of its policies on food and environmental sustainability.

→ National community garden associations and virtual resource centres have sprung up in various places: City Farmer in Vancouver, the Developing Country Farm Radio Network (DCFRN) in Toronto, and the International Network of Resource Centres on Urban Agriculture and Food Security (RUAF) in Leusden, the Netherlands, to name but a few.

It is clearly evident that UA has come to involve an ever-widening range of production systems, technical solutions, actors, and policy instruments.

More importantly, the migration of people from Southern to Northern cities is adding diversity to local values and culture. UA enables many minority groups to connect in a very meaningful way among themselves and with their foreign host culture. Italian immigrants, for example, spearheaded the community gardens movement in Montreal in the 1970s. This translates into more UA, enabling cities to reduce their *ecological footprint*. UA, therefore, can act as a practical entry for our cities into a more sustainable world.

In the South, however, those very countries that have the most to gain from policies positive to UA are, by and large, the ones where such policies are less developed. Over the last 10 to 15 years, however, the picture in the South has changed rapidly. As you will read in this book, more and more governments in Southern countries and cities are revisiting UA. True, the experience of the North bears some relevance, but Southern cities realize they need to innovate and learn from each other — their approach must fit their own conditions, meet their own needs, and fall within their own means. More and more, cities in developing countries are experimenting and sharing their innovations with other cities of the South as well as, increasingly, cities of the North.

This book provides a brief overview of the current state of UA and of IDRC's approach to supporting UA through targeted research. By describing a variety of research projects in diverse settings, the book shows the complex issues at hand as well as their human implications. It examines the lessons provided by the many projects funded through IDRC and its partners and makes some recommendations for future action by the international community as well as by national and municipal bodies. The book concludes by speculating on future directions for UA and assesses its continued role in providing a larger measure of food security for the world's burgeoning cities.

This book, however, is only one element of a much larger "knowledge pyramid," which includes detailed case studies and an extensive range of source materials on urban agriculture, all of which readers are invited to access at **www.idrc.ca/in_focus_cities**.

Luc J.A. Mougeot joined IDRC in late 1989, directing the Urban Environment Management program from 1992 to 1995. In 1996, he founded IDRC's Cities Feeding People program and, from 1996 to 2004, managed over 40 projects on urban agriculture in the developing world. Dr Mougeot is currently a senior program specialist with IDRC's Special Initiatives Division. He holds a doctorate in geography from Michigan State University (1981) and conducted post-doctoral studies in environmental impact assessment in the UK and Germany (1987). From 1978 to 1989, Dr Mougeot was an adjunct professor at the Federal University of Para, Brazil, where he supervised graduate research, served as consultant to development agencies, and coordinated international research projects. He has served as member of various international steering, advisory, editorial, and selection committees on urban agriculture. He is currently a permanent reviewer for the International Science Foundation and sits on the international advisory board for UN-HABITAT's *State of the World Cities Report 2006*. Dr Mougeot has authored or edited over 60 publications, including his most recent, *AGROPOLIS: the Social, Environmental, and Political Dimensions of Urban Agriculture* (Earthscan/IDRC 2005).

Acknowledgments

Over the last 16 years, 11 of which have been at the helm of urban research programs, my work with IDRC has enabled me to meet and learn much from academic researchers, agricultural producers, extension agents, activists, local and national government officials, and senior officers of bilateral and multilateral development agencies. With different expertise and mandates, they all have been grappling with a late 20th century phenomenon for which, in most cases, there is still no clear home, within either their profession or their working environment.

This period in urban history is turning them into true pioneers. To all of them I owe my thanks, having gained first-hand insights into the growth of urban agriculture (UA) worldwide, into the diversity of people engaged and the sheer ingenuity of systems at work, and into the tangible benefits it brings to producers large and small, as well as to others. I have also gained an understanding of the gravity of the constraints and risks that poor producers face and the impact that pro-UA policies can have on a developing-country city.

IDRC owes much to researchers around the world who, over the years, have ably led benchmarking projects and have given life to knowledge networks. With uncommon steadfastness they nurtured teams, advanced the field of research, and collaborated at various levels with policy exercises. Their intellectual integrity and constructive collegiality have already instilled important changes in the attitudes and behaviour of many actors in their cities, countries, or regions. Their respect for the perceptions and responsibilities of other urban actors, their disposition to effectively relate with current policies or to propose new policies for positive changes have made them key artisans of new communities of practice. They include Diana Lee Smith and Davinder Lamba, Camillus Sawio, Gertrude Atukunda and Daniel Maxwell, Joe Nasr, Shingirayi Mushamba and Takawira Mubvami, Safietou Fall and Seydou Niang, Murad Bino, Pay Dreschel, Abdou Fall and Paule Moustier, Lilia Chauca and Julio Moscoso, Mildred Delphin Regis, Pedro Juan del Rosario and Maria Caridad Cruz, Marielle Dubbelling and Alain Santandreu. Henk de Zeeuw, coordinator of the International Network of Resource Centres on Urban Agriculture and Food Security (RUAF), Jac Smit, President of The Urban Agriculture Network, Michael Levenston of City Farmer, David Satterthwaite, formerly Director of the Human Settlements Programme at the International Institute for Environment and Development in London, and Gordon Prain, Coordinator of CGIAR's Urban Harvest, continue to be valued as collaborators and networkers.

Other people have been extremely influential in bringing the results of UA research by IDRC and others to bear on policy agendas and programs of work of several agencies. These include Ulrich Sabell-Koschella at GTZ, Timothy Aldington, Florence Egal, Rachel Nugent, Axel Drescher, Olivio Argenti, Henri Carsalade, and Louise Fresco at FAO, Robert Work, Frank Hartvelt and

Jonas Rabinovitch at UNDP, Joep Bijlmer at DGIS, and Yves Cabannes, Paul Taylor, Dinesh Metah, Chris Radford, Jochen Eigen, Naison Mutizwa, Don Okpala, Christine Auclair, and Lars Reutersward at UNCHS/UN-HABITAT.

Over the years, the Centre has counted on the talent and dedication of an ever-changing team of scientists to sustain, increase, and reinvent IDRC's programing in development research on UA. The Cities Feeding People (CFP) program and its achievements owe very much to the programing work of Luis Navarro, Ola Smith, Naser Faruqui, Denise Deby, Saidou Koala, Carlos Sere, Stephen Tyler, Wardie Leppan, Bertha Mo, Réal Lavergne, Mark Redwood, Brenda-Lee Wilson, Ana Amelia Boischio, and Kristina Taboulchanas. Liliane Castets-Poupart, Wendy Storey, and Karen Trebert supported this team. Many interns over the years have helped CFP to advance its research agenda, whose contributions are recorded in the CFP *Reports* series. Finally, without the institutional and political support of Anne Whyte, Caroline Pestieau, Rohinton Medhora, David Brooks, Joachim Voss, Peter Cooper, and Jean Lebel, CFP would not have achieved as much as it did by 2005. As IDRC's representative on CGIAR, Joachim Voss's advocacy over the years was critical to the eventual launch of the consortium-wide initiative, Urban Harvest.

The final text of this book bears the craftmanship of Bob Stanley. His patience in working and re-working my drafts has earned him a new friend. I wish to thank also the IDRC Communications team, particularly Bill Carman, Kevin Conway, Louise Guénette, and Michelle Hibler, for their genuine interest, preparation of subsidiary case studies, useful reviews, and sound guidance during the development of this manuscript.

This book is dedicated to all the people who are farming the cities of today so that our children and their children can live better in our first urban century.

L.J.A.M.

Part 1

The Issue

Urban agriculture is associated with urban land squatting and is viewed as a socioeconomic problem, not a solution. Authorities are hesitant to be more proactive on UA because it is largely seen as resulting from a failure to address adequately rural development needs.
Mayor Fisho P. Mwale, Lusaka, Zambia

Population shift

Morning has a different sound in the cities of the South than in Northern cities. In the South, roosters compete with the sounds of early morning traffic to announce the new day. Listen carefully, and you may hear goats bleating, cattle lowing, and, as the city wakes, the cries of street vendors offering fresh produce, bread, and other prepared foods.

In the North, there is a clear division between urban and rural. In the South, however, the division is not so clear — agriculture production is not limited to the rural areas. Although it is often frowned upon by the authorities, urban agriculture (UA) is a reality in most Southern cities. In some, it also plays a significant role in providing a measure of food security and income for a rapidly increasing urban population.

The past half-century has seen a massive movement of population in most developing countries. Until the latter half of the 20th century, the developing world was predominantly rural. At the midpoint of the 1900s, fewer than 20% of people in developing countries lived in cities and towns. By the turn of the millennium, that percentage had more than doubled (Figure 1). The US National Research Council estimates that by 2030 more people will be living in urban areas (4.1 billion) than in rural areas (3.1 billion) in middle- and low-income countries. Between now and then nearly all population growth will be in the cities of developing countries, where some cities are growing two or three times faster than the country's overall population. This trend is equivalent to adding a city of one million residents every week (UN-HABITAT 2004).

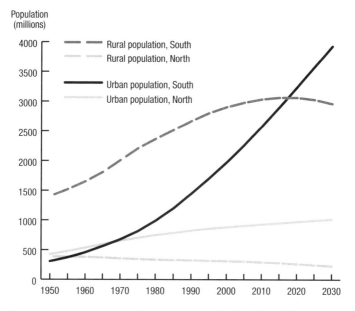

Figure 1. Rural and urban populations in North and South, 1950 to 2030 (projected).
Source: UN (2004).

The phenomenon of rural–urban migration is not unique to the South. In North America and Europe people have been abandoning the rural life since the industrial revolution of the 19th century. The trend accelerated following the Second World War, with the result that about three-quarters of the population in the North is now urban (Figure 1). However, the growth of urban population in the developed world has now slowed to just 0.4% annually, while in developing countries the urban population is growing at an annual rate of 2.3%. In other words, although the North is already far more urban, the urban areas of developing countries are growing much faster — and their populations are larger (UN-HABITAT 2004).

Food: a "basic luxury"

Spectacular as the growth of the cities has been over the past half-century, large cities have existed throughout much of recorded history. For example, more than a thousand years ago, Baghdad was home to more than one million people. About the same time in China, the city of Changan (today called Xi'an) is said to have had 800 000 inhabitants. And if the growth of large cities is nothing new, nor is the practice of urban agriculture.

Archaeologists around the world routinely uncover remains of ingenious large-scale earth and water works in and around the cities of ancient civilizations. There is evidence of agricultural production for a multiplicity of purposes: for food and fodder, building materials, fencing, and even medicinal plants. From the walled gardens of ancient Persia to outposts of the Roman empire in Algeria and Morocco, from Europe's mediaeval monastery towns to the city states of the Aztecs and the terraced farms of Machu Picchu high in the Peruvian Andes, UA thrived (Mougeot 1994). What is new is the scale. Today we have megacities: defined as cities with populations of at least 10 million. Just 30 years ago there were only five megacities. Three of these were in developing countries. The number of megacities is predicted to increase to 23 over the next decade. Nineteen of these cities will be in developing countries. But the megacities represent just the tip of the urban iceberg. Statisticians calculate that by 2015 there will be no fewer than 564 cities around the world with one million or more residents. Of these, 425 will be in developing countries.

One predictable outcome of this massive population shift is urban poverty. Many of the migrants reach the cities with no resources, bringing with them only what they can carry. Employment is generally hard to find, and most of the urban poor live in slums and squatter settlements, without adequate clean water, sanitation, or health care. The global level of urban poverty, currently estimated at 30%, is predicted to grow to 50% by 2020, with nearly all of this growth taking place in the world's less developed countries (UN-HABITAT 2004).

Then there is the question of food. For the urban poor, food has become what can only be termed a "basic luxury." Households from Calcutta to Kinshasa, from Lima to Lagos, spend as much as 80% of their income on food (PCC 1990). In many African cities, it is common for families to eat just one meal a day. Malnutrition and related health issues are commonplace. Little wonder, then, that increasing numbers of people look for ways to supplement the meager amounts of food that they can afford to buy.

Snails and silkworms

In very general terms, urban agriculture can be described as the growing, processing, and distribution of food and nonfood plant and tree crops and the raising of livestock, directly for the urban market, both within and on the fringe of an urban area. It does this through tapping on resources (unused or under-used space, organic waste), services (technical extension, financing, transportation), and products (agrochemicals, tools, vehicles) found in this urban area and, in turn, generates resources (green areas, microclimates, compost), services (catering, recreation, therapy), and products (flowers, poultry, dairy) largely for this urban area (UNDP 1996; Mougeot 2000). The very close connection in space that UA entertains with the ecology and economy of cities makes this very distinct from but complementary to rural agriculture. This description, however, fails to convey the extent of the practice, or the almost infinite variety and sheer ingenuity of techniques employed by urban farmers.

Urban agriculture is typically opportunistic. Its practitioners have evolved and adapted diverse knowledge and know-how to select and locate, farm, process, and market all manner of plants, trees, and livestock. What they have achieved in the very heart of major cities, and dare to pursue despite minimal support, and often in the face of official opposition, is a tribute to human ingenuity. One survey by the United Nations Development Programme (UNDP 1996) identified over 40 farming systems, ranging from horticulture to aquaculture, kitchen gardens to market gardens, and including livestock as varied as cattle, chickens, snails, and silkworms!

Where does all this agriculture take place? Apart from farming in backyards, there is crop and animal production on rooftops, in window boxes, on roadsides, beside railroads, beneath high tension lines, within utility rights of way, in vacant lots of industrial estates, on steep slopes and banks of rivers, and on the grounds of schools, hospitals, prisons, and other institutions. There is aquaculture in tanks, ponds, and pens in rivers. Also, as cities expand, they frequently engulf nearby villages and, in these peri-urban areas, some of the residents continue to farm whatever land is left to them. Some city dwellers even maintain small plots of land on this urban fringe, shuttling out weekly or leaving some family members there to tend the crops during the growing season.

In short, urban agriculture is anywhere and everywhere that people can find even the smallest space to plant a few seeds.

A regular supply of homegrown food can make a considerable difference to the lives of the urban poor. It not only contributes to improved nutritional health but also may free up some of a family's cash income for nonfood expenses such as education.

Not all urban agriculture is carried on at the subsistence level as a temporary necessity by recent immigrants from rural areas. It also includes commercial operations producing food in greenhouses and other spaces, but is more often small-scale and scattered around the city. The produce is usually processed and marketed by the producers and their families.

Women's roles

It is unrealistic to expect cities can ever become self-sufficient in food. Most cereal crops can be grown efficiently only in the rural areas. But there is no question that urban agriculture already makes a significant contribution to food security in many major cities. The UNDP estimates perhaps as many as 800 million urban farmers produce about 15% of the world's food. That goes a long way toward reducing the food insecurity of vulnerable groups of people.

Women and children are always among the most vulnerable, so it comes as no surprise that it is often women who predominate in urban food production. Urban agriculture, as a means of improving food security — and earning extra income — is particularly attractive to women as it allows them to work close to their homes and to provide extra food to improve the nutritional status of their children. Any surplus may be sold, and the income used to improve living conditions or even to invest in more profitable small enterprises, processing and marketing city-grown products.

However, women often face difficulties accessing land, water, labour, capital, technologies, and other services. In most countries, they likely have received less education than men and, in some countries, they are prevented by laws, customs, and attitudes from owning assets or even from making decisions about how any assets are to be used. A woman is also expected to maintain the home, prepare food, and care for the children, the sick, and the elderly. All of which too often limits their ability to contribute more to urban food production (Hovorka 1999).

Despite these restrictions, women do find ways to succeed in the business of urban agriculture, sometimes even dominating the trade of produce that is grown by urban farmers. Women will buy directly from producers and either resell in smaller quantities or process the produce and sell prepared foods. The most successful women act as "bankers" for the agricultural producers, providing cash advances to farmers to ensure continuing supplies.

Easing ecological problems

As urban areas grow in population, they expand outward, often overwhelming the natural environment, destroying ecosystems, and drawing resources from well beyond their defined limits. Cities' dependence on massive and relentless imports of food, energy, and other resources from distant areas, and often on exports of their wastes to those areas, can also be destructive. The city's ecological footprint has long been a problem in the cities of the North (Rees 1997). Now, the rapid and usually unplanned growth of many cities in developing countries, coupled with rising consumption levels, is also putting a strain on the natural resource base of the South.

Urban agriculture alone will not solve the ecological problems of growing cities, but it does help to protect the environment in a variety of ways. For example, in many cities urban farmers make productive use of many organic waste products, turning them into soil-enhancing mulch. Wastewater can be used to irrigate crops. By cultivating every available piece of open space — even rooftops — urban farmers contribute to the greening of the city, helping to reduce pollution and improve air quality. Even the fact that less food has to be trucked in to the city contributes to sustainability and has a positive environmental impact. Urban agriculture helps to reduce a city's ecological footprint even as the city continues to grow (Nelson 1996).

Coupled with an improved environment is an overall improvement in the health of the urban population. A more livable city is a healthier city. For the urban poor in particular, the availability of fresh vegetables and other foods coupled with increased opportunities for income means improved overall health, and perhaps the opportunity to break out of the cycle of poverty.

An uncertain existence

Sadly, the sound of a rooster crowing at dawn is not music to all ears. In many developing country cities urban agriculture is not just frowned upon, it is illegal. Because it is spontaneous and uncontrolled, many city planners and municipal governments view UA as an unsightly problem. This attitude is often a hangover from the colonial era when Europeans attempted to reproduce an urban environment more suited to northern climates — complete with European-style rules and regulations that remain on the books today.

One result of this situation is that urban farmers in many cities are constantly harassed by officials and the police. Agricultural activity in urban areas almost always contravenes some zoning regulation or by-law. Parks were never intended as grazing grounds for livestock, and the owners of vacant land are rarely pleased to see it sprouting corn and beans. So action is demanded, and sometimes taken, although the degree to which the rules are enforced may depend to some extent on the current need for food.

Nevertheless, periodic harassment adds to what for many is already an uncertain existence and dissuades many food producers from investing extra time or resources in their operations. This is particularly true for the poorest urban farmers, especially women, who are liable at any time to be forced out of business by wealthier or more powerful groups, or by land speculators. The poor have little recourse in such situations, since their operations were probably illegal in the first place.

There are other issues around urban agriculture that are potentially much more serious. There are health risks as well as health benefits. Risks can arise from the over-use of pesticides by inexperienced or illiterate workers. Women and children working the farm plots are often at greatest risk of pesticide poisoning. There is also the risk of human exposure to contaminants and pathogens as a result of farming operations in the city. Keeping livestock in the city raises the possibility of zoonotic diseases — diseases that can be transmitted from animals and birds to humans (such as avian flu). In the densely populated urban environment, such diseases could spread rapidly and be extremely difficult to control.

There are health risks too for urban farmers who grow crops on contaminated lands, as well as for those who consume the produce from those lands. Typically it is the poor, the recent arrivals in the city, who must make use of such undesirable locations. Similarly, where water is scarce, as it often is, the urban farmer may irrigate crops with untreated wastewater. Again the health risks are high: according to the World Health Organization (WHO) dirty water is by far the largest environmental killer around the world. Once again, women and children, who do much of the fieldwork, are at greatest risk.

Increasing recognition

Urban agriculture is here to stay. In fact, as we have seen, it never really went away. Today some enlightened city administrations are embracing the concept rather than attempting to stifle it. Cooperation and control rather than opposition and restriction can maximize the benefits of UA while minimizing the problems. This can clearly be seen in and around some Asian cities, where UA has had a long tradition. Far from banning the practice, policymakers and planners have encouraged food production as a critical urban function. Many Chinese urban municipalities are intentionally oversized to allow room for a city "foodshed."

In Africa and Latin America too, there is increasing recognition of the value of urban agriculture, and many cities are attempting to find positive ways to tackle the issues. Regardless, city governments are faced with two certainties. First, people will still keep moving to the cities, and many of them will find ways to grow at least a little food. Second, if city governments adopt policies that encourage UA, the number of urban farmers will likely increase substantially. Clearly, UA must be viewed not as a problem but as one tool contributing to sustainable urban development, and conventional strategies for urban food security need to be reassessed in view of its potential role.

Urban agriculture is increasingly on the international agenda, recognized as a key part of a comprehensive solution to the problems of the runaway growth of cities in developing countries. International donor agencies are now more willing to fund research to better understand the phenomenon and find ways to make UA more effective, safer, and more responsive to the needs of the urban population. But it has been noted that even where the political environment is open to UA, frequently the policy structure is not. Thus there is a pressing need to develop methodology for relating research and policy to fully exploit the comparative advantages of both rural and urban areas.

Cities Feeding People

Canada's International Development Research Centre (IDRC) has been a pioneer in promoting the importance of urban agriculture. In 1983, IDRC became the first major international agency to undertake formal research in the field when it funded a study of six urban centres at the Mazingira Institute in Nairobi, Kenya. In the decade that followed, IDRC expanded its interest in the emerging field, and that interest became a commitment to research and development in urban food systems and related issues. The program was called Cities Feeding People (CFP). Over the last decade, CFP has supported many research projects in Africa, Latin America, and the Middle East, some of them jointly funded with other international donors. The next part of this book examines the rationale and summarizes the evolution of IDRC's approach to urban agriculture research over the past two decades.

Part 2

The Approach

On the Web

THE RESEARCH

Some bilateral aid agencies have urban agriculture assistance programmes. The International Development Research Centre (IDRC) of Canada is the most notable.
UNDP (1996, p. 151)

In September 2000, the United Nations Millennium Declaration set out eight Millennium Development Goals. These were designed to provide the international community with an expanded vision of development and a framework for measuring development progress. First among those goals: eradicate extreme poverty and hunger.

Urban agriculture contributes directly to this goal. Without doubt, the two major forces driving the poorest city dwellers to become urban farmers are the critical need for a reliable source of fresh food and the hope of improving their precarious financial circumstances (Mougeot 2005). It can also be argued that UA contributes — directly or indirectly — to three of the remaining Millennium Development Goals: reduce child mortality, improve maternal health, and ensure environmental sustainability.

IDRC's commitment to UA research began long before the start of the new millennium. IDRC has had some involvement in research on urban food systems almost since it was established in 1970 and was the first major international donor agency to give formal recognition to UA. From an early emphasis on food security, nutrition, and the treatment and reuse of organic waste, research expanded to include urban food processing and distribution, then urban food production itself. Formal research on UA at IDRC covers a period of 20 years, from 1984 to 2004. During those two decades, IDRC has disbursed some (CA) $9 million on over 90 related projects in more than 40 countries.

An evolving approach

IDRC's approach to UA is best viewed in three distinct phases, beginning with the years from 1984 to 1992. The report of the UN World Commission on Environment and Development, *Our Common Future,* was probably the first major UN publication to highlight the potential of UA as a tool for sustainable urban development (Brundtland 1987). But perhaps of more direct influence on IDRC's agenda was the UN Food–Energy Nexus Programme, whose field surveys noted the widespread practice of urban fuelwood and food production in the developing world (Sachs 1988). University of Hong Kong geographer Dr Yue-Man Yeung, one of the authors of the surveys, joined IDRC during this period, and organized a fact-finding workshop on UA in Singapore in 1984.

IDRC's programs on agriculture, health, and urban development at this time funded small projects, largely isolated one from another. Research on UA became the latest emphasis in IDRC's work on urban food systems, with its focus mostly on food production. The research was not clearly linked with — much less embedded in — any public policy process. Raising public awareness was the main nonacademic aim. Even so, results from some of this initial research would eventually lead to more action-oriented research, including practical technology and policy interventions.

Benchmarking this period is the Mazingira Institute's statistical survey of agricultural production in six Kenyan cities (Lee-Smith et al. 1987). This was the first study in any country to estimate the size and worth of major urban crop and animal production systems. It has since inspired many other surveys and its widely published results are still used.

From 1993 to 1996, IDRC's approach to UA evolved as a result of its interaction with UNDP's LIFE program, global survey, and 1996 book on UA entitled *Urban Agriculture: Food, Jobs and Sustainable Cities*. IDRC was involved in developing the book and was invited by UNDP to lead the follow-up to the book's recommendations with other agencies. A major international workshop was held in Ottawa in 1993 to launch the UA component of IDRC's new Urban Environment Management program and to help develop a research agenda.

A significant shift in IDRC's approach in the first period was that more of the new or follow-up projects were actually driven by and supported specific local policy interventions or technology interventions. Responsiveness, timing, and partnering became critical. Research grants on urban food production were now larger, run by institutions, implemented by multidisciplinary research teams. They used participatory methods, secured parallel funding from other sources, and shared localized policy and technology outcomes.

Also of significance, an in-depth survey in Latin America and the Caribbean led to the creation in 1995 of the Latin American Research Network on Urban Agriculture (AGUILA), and broadened the geographical spread of projects (Prudencio 1997). The projects were still city-specific, however, with little interaction among them. There was no formal networking effort outside of

Latin America and the Caribbean, and little capacity building beyond some individual graduate research grants.

With increased emphasis on action-oriented research, IDRC also stepped up its engagement in international advocacy for partnerships with UN agencies, bilateral organizations, and foundations. This took various forms, including visits, interviews and presentations, papers in conferences of specific interest groups, and sessions at international summits in Istanbul, Nairobi, New York, Québec, Rome, and Washington, DC. This helped IDRC to develop a rapport based on trust and collaboration with individuals and units within international agencies.

Some benchmarks of this period:

➤ Funded by UN-HABITAT/UNDP's Sustainable Cities Programme, IDRC's programing on UA in the Sustainable Dar es Salaam Project was featured at the UN's Habitat II Conference in Istanbul in 1996.

➤ The IDRC book *Cities Feeding People* (Egziabher et al. 1994) and a special issue of the *African Urban Quarterly* on urban agriculture in Africa (Mougeot 1999) collected the results from early IDRC-supported research. The new CFP *Reports* series was created and references started to appear in UN agency reports and newsletters.

➤ IDRC convened and created an informal Support Group on Urban Agriculture (SGUA) in Ottawa in 1996 to follow up on UNDP's book recommendations. In doing so, it expanded beyond largely North America-based think tanks to include other Canadian and European-based agencies and international NGOs.

Cities Feeding People

IDRC programing on UA came of age in 1997 with the creation of the Cities Feeding People (CFP) program, which evolved through two 4-year phases to 2004. A banner international event that was pivotal to CFP's work in this period was UNDP's Colloquium of Mayors on Governance for Sustainable Growth and Equity, during which IDRC and SGUA organized a round table of mayors on UA. This triggered a series of policy-oriented projects in partnership with UN-HABITAT's Urban Management Programme (UMP) and affiliates in Latin America, the Caribbean, and East and Central Africa.

IDRC also lobbied successfully for the mainstreaming of UA programing at the UN's Food and Agriculture Organization (FAO) (COAG-FAO 1999). It pressed for, advised, and funded a new global initiative on UA by the Consultative Group on International Agriculture Research (CGIAR), now called Urban Harvest (CIP 1999). Largely through Urban Harvest's Nairobi office, IDRC increased its outreach in sub-Saharan Africa, bringing UA expertise to bear on fledgling policy initiatives in major East African cities.

Program delivery was organized around five "pillars" of activity:

1. **Research** — Moved from single-city to multicity projects; developed regional networks in Latin America and the Caribbean and in West and Central Africa, with groundwork for a third network in East and Southern Africa.

2. **Training** — Saw the launch of AGROPOLIS, a program of graduate field research awards, to streamline graduate training (see page 19); designed and initiated a series of regional training courses for researchers and city managers, and used internships to explore UA issues on which more knowledge was needed to inform policy and technology actions.

3. **Information** — Developed a large, content-rich Web site; cofunded (with DGIS) and managed a global information network on UA, the Resource Centre on Urban Agriculture and Forestry (RUAF), whose resources include bibliographies, directories, expert consultations, e-conferences, and *Urban Agriculture Magazine*, which is published in five languages.

On the Web
THE RESEARCH

4. Evaluation — Carried out evaluations in Latin America and the Caribbean and in sub-Saharan Africa and introduced a standard contract clause with recipients for self-monitoring and reporting on project impacts.

5. Results utilization — Began to record systematically who used project findings for what purpose, how this was done and with what results — this has affected project design and implementation, field monitoring by IDRC and other funding institutions, evaluations, and program-level reporting.

From the outset, CFP was designed to be responsive, flexible, and demand-driven. The goal was to support development research that "seeks to remove constraints and enhance the potential for UA to improve household food security, income generation, and public health, as well as the management of waste, water, and land, for the benefit of the urban poor." Clearly this was not a goal that any one agency — let alone one with the limited resources of IDRC — could hope to achieve working in isolation. Recognizing this, CFP found ways to encourage and collaborate with other donor organizations, as well as with academic institutions and NGOs.

The program also encouraged governments at all levels to recognize the benefits that UA brings to producers, consumers, and the city itself, and to tackle problems in a constructive way, especially the issues that are preventing UA from realizing its full potential as an industry. This frequently involved bringing researchers, politicians, and technocrats together with the producers to develop effective policies and practical solutions.

It is possible that CFP's most lasting legacy will be as a convener, an advocate, and a facilitator of partnerships for advancing both practice and policy on UA. Cities have been encouraged to learn from each other's experiences and to form national and even regional networks. For example, in April 2000, delegations from 20 Latin American cities met in Quito, Ecuador, to debate the

A Meaningful Impact on Development

Because the field of UA has only recently gained recognition in most countries, there is a real shortage of research at the local level. The AGROPOLIS awards program helped to overcome that shortage by supporting innovative graduate research that adds to the body of knowledge on UA in developing countries (Mougeot 2005). All this research was field-based and was carried out in close affiliation with one or several local nonacademic actors, which pledged support and intended to use results.

The program, which was launched in 1998, has provided more than 50 grants to researchers in Africa, Latin America, and Asia. AGROPOLIS awards supported field research that runs the gamut from studying use of crop residues to feed goats, to the benefits of worm compost, to the effects of gender on commercial urban agriculture systems. The awards covered periods of up to18 months, depending on the level of research proposed.

Frequently, the research was designed and implemented in collaboration with partners such as community-based organizations, NGOs, city councils and government departments. Above all, AGROPOLIS gave students an opportunity to have their graduate research make a meaningful impact on development. Here are just three examples of how AGROPOLIS awardees have had an impact on official policies regarding UA:

- In Gaborone, Botswana, Alice Hovorka worked with the Ministry of Agriculture to organize a national workshop and a task force on peri-urban farming, and worked with officials to draft a UA policy paper.

- In Zaria, Nigeria, Chuo Adamu Nsangu carried out a study in conjunction with Ahmadu Bello University and the Zaria Department of Urban and Regional Planning to assess urban land use policies relating to UA and made recommendations for physical planning based on the patterns and characteristics of UA in the city.

- In Kampala, Uganda, Grace Nabulo's research into the heavy metal content of crops grown on polluted sites across the city informed new city ordinances (2005) designed to ensure food safety by prohibiting food production on industrial waste sites and other contaminated lands.

Administered by IDRC, AGROPOLIS was a component of the Global Initiative of SGUA, which is sponsored by FAO, UNDP, and the Netherlands Directorate General for International Cooperation.

On the Web
THE RESEARCH

policy experience and potential of UA. CFP helped to design and sponsor the event, was an active participant, and committed to several follow-up activities.

At the end of the conference, all the mayors signed a series of resolutions and recommendations now known as the Quito Declaration and committed to form a working group of cities on UA. Since that event the number of cities that have signed on to the declaration has tripled to more than 50.

Building capacity — and bridges

By creating opportunities for government policymakers and technocrats to receive additional training, CFP promoted integration of UA into the urban planning process. Such training has provided both the awareness and the knowledge needed to maximize the benefits of UA while minimizing the negative aspects.

Cities Feeding People occupied a unique niche in the international development community as the only program focused on supporting applied research designed to tackle the problems and needs of urban producers. It encouraged partners to work across disciplines using participatory and consultative processes and convened groups to bring together innovative technologies and policy changes. It lent support to national and regional networks that strengthen South–South cooperation. Above all, it took every opportunity to bring people's perspectives into the technology and policy-making processes by working directly with the stakeholders.

The program focused on strengthening those links between research results and the development of policies that encourage and manage the growth of UA. This focus derives from CFP's specific objectives:

➤ To strengthen local research capacity and generate information on UA at the household and community level so that cities can formulate and implement policy and technology options, primarily for the benefit of the urban poor;

➤ To mobilize and enhance regional capacities to share experiences in UA, identify common policy and technology obstacles, and share and adapt solutions through training and networking; and

➤ To influence governments, policymakers, and international agencies to effectively incorporate UA into their development programs.

However, to take full advantage of the economic and environmental benefits that properly managed UA offers, many questions still need to be answered.

➤ What policies and technologies offer the best tools to improve the food security of the poorest city dwellers?

➤ What mix of crop and livestock choice and growing practices offers the best balance of nutritional value, safety, and work effort?

➤ How much does gender influence the urban farmer's ability to succeed in improving the family's nutrition?

➤ What tenure arrangements can be offered that will allow organized groups, particularly women and the very poor, to have equitable access to urban spaces for agriculture?

➤ What role does agricultural biodiversity play in urban farming, and is there a role for genetically modified organisms (GMOs)?

➤ What innovative forms of credit can be made available to assist urban producers and small-scale processing operations?

In attempting to find answers to these and other questions, IDRC works closely with three crucial groups of urban actors — research institutions, public agencies, and urban producers' organizations — and focuses on policies, practices, and technologies. In the process, it has helped to bring UA research into the mainstream by working

On the Web
THE RESEARCH

closely with international development organizations, UN agencies, local government agencies, and NGOs.

Perhaps most important, many projects have helped to build bridges — enabling urban farmers to be heard in official policy circles and to gain better access to public resources and services.

Maximizing impact

Many of the research projects supported by CFP were undertaken by national or international NGOs. It was recognized, however, that some level of government involvement was essential for research to succeed in bringing about changes in official attitudes and policies. Thus, in Latin America and Africa, government and nongovernment researchers have collaborated to varying degrees on a wide range of projects, some led by NGOs, others by government agencies.

For example, in Harare, Zimbabwe, a survey of urban food producers conducted by an NGO led to a forum for policymakers and eventually resulted in local policy initiatives to better manage UA. In Kampala, Uganda, findings from a research institute survey were used to argue for the integration of UA in the city's urban development plan, leading to new zoning provisions and the adoption of new city by-laws. And in Dakar, Senegal, it was an NGO study of wastewater management that led to a ministers' conference on UA and subsequently to legislative proposals in the national parliament.

In each of these examples events did not move quickly — taking a decade or more to reach the goal of improving policies for UA. The creation of regional networks that bring together representatives of cities as well as local and national governments, as in the Quito example, maximized the impact of the research results. In 2003, a Ministers' Conference on Urban and Peri-urban Agriculture (UPA) was held in Harare, Zimbabwe. The event was convened by a regional NGO, the Municipal Development Partnership for East and Southern Africa (MDP-ESA), and sponsored in part by IDRC. At the end of the conference, all the participating nations signed the Harare Declaration strongly supporting the promotion of UPA.

Subsequent events in Zimbabwe have shown that support for the Declaration has gone beyond mere words. After some discussion with authorities, urban farmers were spared the evictions that otherwise forced many informal traders and families living in irregular settlements to leave the city of Harare.

The way ahead

Over a period of 20 years, and particularly over the last decade, IDRC's approach to UA matured into a well-orchestrated strategy. This used human expertise, financial resources, and institutional networks to tackle gaps in knowledge or capacity that stand in the way of urban agriculture's contribution to healthier, more prosperous, equitable, and sustainable cities.

With the completion of the second phase of CFP in 2004, IDRC's support for UA research continues as part of a new program on Urban Poverty and Environment. It takes an integrated approach to environmental and natural resources issues in cities, with particular emphasis on UA, water, and sanitation. It will also support research on waste management and vulnerabilities to natural disasters, with land tenure as a cross-cutting issue.

In Part 3 we will take a more detailed look at a number of the research projects supported by IDRC in the cities of Africa, Latin America and the Caribbean, and the Middle East. We will also meet some of the people who are on the front line to ensure that UA is integrated into the fabric of city life in a manner that is both sustainable and effective in improving the lives of city dwellers.

On the Web
THE RESEARCH

Part 3

Experiences from the Field

*UA has several advantages in Kampala. It increases urban food
security, produce from rural areas is expensive and less fresh,
and it creates sources of income. UA also reduces open space
maintenance costs to local government.*
Mayor Christopher Iga, Kampala, Uganda

On the Web

THE RESEARCH

Blurring the boundaries

When you first hear it, the term "urban agriculture" sounds like
a contradiction. Most of us, particularly in the North, are condi-
tioned to think of agriculture as an activity that happens in rural
areas, not in towns and cities. As we saw in Part 1, however,
there is in reality no tidy dividing line where agricultural activity
ends — although some city planners might wish it were that way
and might still perceive spaces of food production as nonurban,
making them by implication "somebody else's problem." And just

as UA blurs the boundaries between city and country, so the issues invoked by city farming overlap and interconnect.

This brief review of some of the UA projects supported by IDRC offers a cross-section of the major issues confronting UA in Latin America, the Caribbean, Africa, and the Middle East, with the emphasis on policy-based research. However, because the issues are frequently interrelated, many of the projects supported by IDRC have multiple objectives, seeking solutions to a problem at both the technical and the policy level.

Land, people, and policies

The availability of land for urban agriculture — and access to it — are crucial issues in most cities of the developing world. Insecure land tenure can lead to conflicts, sometimes violent ones, and municipalities that recognize the potential benefits of UA wrestle with outdated regulations in an effort to bring some order to this growing urban enterprise.

Two streams of projects in sub-Saharan Africa illustrate the evolution of IDRC's approach to policy research on UA in the 1990s — but first a little background. Daniel Maxwell and Samuel Zziwa, the principal researchers on a project in Kampala, wrote that the 1980s had witnessed the collapse of much of the formal, modern sector of Africa's economy, with plummeting standards of living for both urban and rural people. Programs designed in the 1960s and 1970s to ground rural population in rural areas clearly were not successful, and structural adjustment in the late 1980s forced the cancellation of many of these programs.

Cities were burgeoning despite the lack of official attention to their problems, most of all unemployment. In Uganda, the Amin regime brought the collapse of much large-scale enterprise, to be replaced by an underground economy. Kampala's annual growth rate neared 9% and the city population had doubled to nearly a million by 1990 (Maxwell and Zziwa 1992). In Tanzania, attempts at rural repatriation in the mid-1980s proved unenforceable and politically very unpopular. And Dar es Salaam, the largest city, kept growing amidst a deteriorating urban environment.

IDRC started supporting projects in both cities at a time when awareness was growing in some political sectors that UA had become an important component of the informal sector of these cities. In 1993, IDRC and UN-HABITAT agreed to cosupport the Sustainable Dar es Salaam Project (SDP). The project was to lead to a new strategic urban development plan for the city, and policies for integrating UA into improved management of the city's environment. In many ways, SDP exemplified IDRC's shift from academic to policy-oriented research on UA during the early 1990s. This was the first IDRC project on UA to be formally and systematically embedded in a public policy process. Other stakeholders in the project included the City of Dar es Salaam and the Ministry of Urban Development, and the Minister himself had asked that SDP devote one of its working groups to UA issues.

Dr Camillus Sawio, a geographer from the University of Dar es Salaam, had just completed an IDRC-funded dissertation at Clark University (Sawio 1993). His topic was UA in Dar es Salaam, making him a natural choice to lead the project team of six Tanzanian researchers. The team informed and advised several working groups on issues such as access to (and use of) urban land, food safety, and waste management.

Based on a survey of nearly 2 000 urban producers, the researchers documented the main UA production systems, the areas used, the numbers of people involved, main crops and types of livestock, and operations of various sizes. They looked at trends over the previous 5 years, as well as related issues of transportation, irrigation, inputs, waste management, marketing, and related infrastructure, prices, and practices (Kyessi 1996). The researchers scrutinized the interactions — both beneficial and detrimental — between UA and the urban environment as well as the role UA was

On the Web
THE RESEARCH

already playing (and might play) in using the municipality's solid and liquid wastes. It noted producers' use of agrochemicals and their recycling of agricultural wastes (Kishimba 1996).

Most importantly, the researchers studied city by-laws and other "instruments of intervention" that have some impact on UA. They gathered recommendations from the urban farmers themselves on which activities should be allowed or promoted, which should be prohibited or strictly regulated, and why. They critiqued the adequacy and enforceability of by-laws, and offered advice and assistance in revising them and writing new ones. Thus the project gave a voice to urban producers, a group still notably ignored in most urban policy exercises worldwide (Mwaiselage 1996). By the time SDP was completed in 1997, nine other Tanzanian municipalities were preparing to replicate the process — a clear sign of the project's impact.

The project team also created an information base to assist in the management of open spaces, recreational areas, and hazard-prone lands. The team's findings contributed to a successful proposal for the rehabilitation of urban garden centres. The proposal secured half a million US dollars from the National Income Generating Program. And, by 1997 several propositions for the new Strategic Urban Development Plan of Dar es Salaam had been adopted (Sawio 1998).

Real progress in three African cities

Resolving conflicts over access to and use of urban land was one of the key management issues identified by SDP. This issue became the focus of a subsequent three-city project that included Kinondoni (one of three municipalities that constitute the city of Dar es Salaam), Kampala, and Harare. The project proposal came from an NGO, the Municipal Development Partnership for Eastern and Southern Africa (MDP-ESA), following a workshop with researchers and public policy agencies from Tanzania, Uganda, and Zimbabwe (MDP-ESA 2001, 2002).

The researchers highlighted both similarities and differences in the approach to UA in the three cities. Kampala, which a decade earlier had a relatively limited policy framework for UA, had progressed significantly. The 30-year-old Kampala Structure Plan was revised to include UA as a legitimate land use. To implement the new approach, an Urban Agriculture Unit was set up in the Production and Marketing Department of Kampala City Council (relocated from the Ministry of Agriculture). A participatory process for writing new by-laws was begun, and new regulations calling for occupancy licences and registration for urban producers were created to provide more secure tenure to a greater number of people than before (Nuwagaba et al. 2005). The situation was similar in Harare, which had a record of regulatory and planning steps providing for agricultural land use on private and public land, but had found itself ill-equipped to cope with the large-scale growth in recent decades. Unofficially, the large-scale practice of UA is now widely accepted, and the city council has begun to change its attitude, partly as a result of information provided by this and previous research projects. The researchers found few citywide formal mechanisms for conflict resolution, but proposed Parliamentary legislation would explicitly empower local governments to regulate UA (Mudimu et al. 2005).

Only in Kinondoni was UA widely supported and practiced so that it has become accepted as a feature in the city. There were policies and regulations governing UA, and the municipality's Web site even contains information about different types of agriculture in and around the city, as well as photos of urban farmers at work. Of the three cities, Kinondoni had the more advanced legal and regulatory framework but, as in Harare, there was no participatory strategy for its revision or for compliance. Village elders and village courts were the main local mechanism used for conflict resolution (Mlozi et al. 2005). In his report on the project, Takawira Mubvami (2004) comments: "There is a need to identify institutional arrangements ... to manage conflict, negotiate, prevent, and resolve disputes on accessing land between

farmers and authorities, and between farming households."
Interviews with hundreds of farmers in all three cities revealed
that the most common means of accessing land were informal
ones, typically, either squatting on unoccupied public or private
land or borrowing land from relations or friends. Renting is
increasingly beyond the reach of poor families as speculation
pushes up land values in the cities. In all three cities, researchers
found that demand for land suitable for UA outstripped supply —
yet aerial photography of districts close to the Dar es Salaam city
centre showed plenty of suitable vacant land.

In both Kampala and Harare research revealed that planning and
land-use legislation fails to address the land tenure issue — planners simply did not recognize UA as a legal land use. However, the
researchers did find that both cities had started looking at issues
of UA in a "positive manner." Kinondoni, on the other hand,
introduced Urban Farming Regulations in 1992 but then failed
to do much with them. "The application and enforcement of
these regulations has been very weak, resulting in a haphazard
approach to UA, which is not integrated with land use planning,"
notes Mubvami.

Complicating the issue was the fact that most of the urban farmers were simply not aware of legislation and policies governing
UA. "In Harare for example, the local authority has been applying
these by-laws and policies intermittently ... making it very difficult for the farmers to have an appreciation for how serious the
local authority is," Mubvami writes. He adds that in all three
cities regulations and laws have not been widely circulated and
need to be simplified to ensure that the urban farmers can fully
understand them. In Kampala a participatory by-law formulation
process, assisted by the CGIAR Urban Harvest initiative and supported by IDRC and the UK's Department for International Development (DFID), began addressing this need in 2004. (KUFSALC and
UH 2005; Nuwagaba et al. 2005).

With some legal and policy framework in place in the three cities, Mubvami's report concludes that what is urgently needed is a clearer integration of UA into land-use planning procedures. In the telling words of one former director of the Dar es Salaam Planning Department: "Urban planners have had no problem in setting aside land to bury the dead. Should not we, with more reason, set aside land which will actually enable people to feed themselves and stay alive."

There are many signs of progress, however. At a 2003 Ministers' Conference on Urban and Peri-urban Agriculture (UPA) in East and Southern Africa, Crispen Maseva, the senior ecologist in Zimbabwe's Natural Resources Department, commented: "With the growing acknowledgement of the permanency of UPA, not necessarily in location-specific terms but rather as a feature of the urban socioeconomic fabric and landscape, official responses to and treatment of UPA have begun to noticeably shift" (Mushamba et al. 2003).

On the Web
THE RESEARCH

City partners in Latin America

One region where IDRC and its partners have had considerable success in advancing the integration of UA into city planning is Latin America and the Caribbean (LAC). Approximately 75% of the region's people now live in urban areas. As in Africa, globalization and market liberalization, often reinforced by structural adjustment or other national policies, directly affected livelihoods in the 1980s and 1990s. This has been further aggravated by unemployment and a decline in real wages. Little wonder, then, that many in the cities resort to informal activities to survive. Urban food production, processing, and marketing are among these strategies (Cabannes and Mougeot 1999).

As elsewhere, access to land and land tenure limit the effective development of UA. Rapid population increase and land speculation are forcing the price of land and land rents well beyond the

IDRC's Partners

Ten years ago, IDRC became the first international agency to launch a full-scale program dedicated to research on urban agriculture. Today, it is no longer alone. There is now a veritable alphabet of regional and global organizations with similar objectives, many of which are partners with IDRC in a range of projects.

At the top of the list is SGUA, the Support Group on Urban Agriculture. Founded in 1996 at a meeting hosted by IDRC, SGUA is a global initiative with 43 members that focuses on research training, policy, technical assistance, credit, and investment. It also publishes the *Urban Agriculture Magazine* three times a year. SGUA also launched the AGROPOLIS awards program, which was administered by IDRC.

The information arm of the SGUA is RUAF, the Resource Centre on Urban Agriculture and Forestry, which was created to ease the integration of UA into the policies and plans of municipal authorities. The first phase of RUAF was administered through CFP. At the end of this phase. RUAF created a foundation that now administers its second phase, also funded by IDRC.

Urban Harvest is the new name for the program of technical research on UA created by CGIAR, the Consultative Group on International Agricultural Research. Urban Harvest is headed by CIP, the International Potato Centre, a CGIAR member with headquarters in Peru.

For the United Nations, there is the UN-HABITAT (formerly UNCHS, United Nations Centre for Human Settlements), The UN's Sustainable Cities Programme is part of UN-HABITAT. FAO, the UN Food and Agriculture Organization, has set up a Priority Area for Interdisciplinary Action on Food in the Cities.

Regionally, there is AGUILA, the Latin American Research Network on Urban Agriculture. Established with assistance from IDRC, AGUILA forms strategic alliances with city governments that have committed to the promotion of UA by signing the Quito Declaration. In francophone West Africa, there is the French-speaking Network for Urban Agriculture in West and Central Africa coordinated by IAGU, the Institut africain de gestion urbaine. In East and Southern Africa there is the Urban Agriculture Program of MDP-ESA.

reach of the urban poor. However, IDRC projects found that **land availability** was less of an issue than access to **suitable land**, and until recently UA was still largely ignored in municipal land-use planning in most cities of the region. Even highly urbanized municipalities have extensive undeveloped or partially built-up land and water areas that could be used for agriculture (Table 1).

In the search for solutions, IDRC supported a regional project that linked 10 cities in Argentina, Brazil, Cuba, Ecuador, Honduras, Mexico, and Uruguay. The project was cofunded by UMP-LAC of UN-HABITAT and the Peruvian Institute for the Promotion of Sustainable Development (IPES), a regional NGO. The project studied **how** UA policy was being developed locally, **who** the urban farmers were, and **what** barriers they faced in growing food and raising livestock. Researchers documented innovative local approaches, ranging from cultural preservation and control of urban sprawl, to fiscal incentives aimed at revitalizing the local economy, to small-scale agroindustries and creation of national UA programs (UMP-LAC 2001).

The project also encouraged formal and informal interaction among local authorities. One unexpected but much welcomed outcome of this interaction was the Quito Declaration, a powerful statement in support of UA signed by the mayors of over

Table 1. Open-space area within city limits in four cities of Latin America.

City (population)	Open-space area	Observations
Quito, Ecuador (1.4 million in 2001)	35% in 2001	Suitability not assessed
Rosario, Argentina (0.9 million in 2001)	80% in 2003	Largely suitable
Santiago de los Caballeros, Dominican Republic (0.5 million in 2002)	33% in 1998	Plus another 16% used for UA
Cienfuegos, Cuba (141 000 in 2002)	10% in 2003	Plus another 8% used for UA

Source: IDRC project results.

50 cities. This followed an international seminar on UA in Quito, Ecuador, cosponsored by IDRC and FAO as part of the project.

The combined experiences of the 10 cities provided many of the elements for a new policy framework. A new, three-city project was undertaken by UMP-LAC and IPES with IDRC support. The objective was to design and test planning tools and methods that cities in the region would need to apply the action plan produced by the 10-city project. The cities, differing in size and circumstances, but all with some level of official recognition of UA, were Rosario, Argentina, Cienfuegos, Cuba, and Governador Valadares, Brazil.

The three cities formed multidisciplinary teams that included local government officials, universities, researchers, community members, farmers, and local NGOs. The teams developed a land-use mapping system, as well as practical tools, policies, and strategies for integrating UA into land-use planning. In addition to making recommendations on the need for a legal framework governing UA and the integration of agriculture into urban land-use planning, they tackled issues such as the need for alternative credit systems to assist urban farmers and the impact of UA on the city environment (UMP-LAC 2003).

The resulting case studies helped draft or improve local policies for UA and the sustainable management of cities. The project has not only contributed to UN-HABITAT campaigns for secure land tenure and good governance, it has also helped to advance the design of new urban settlements that incorporate UA. The project has attracted worldwide interest from such diverse bodies as the Department of Housing of Rosario, Brazil's National Movement of Struggle for Housing, China's Planning Academy, and the Movement of the Homeless in Africa.

Finally, analysis of the 10-city project led to the development of a regional plan for UA, and Quito was chosen as the site for implementing the plan, making it a sort of UA regional laboratory. The program has brought community members together with municipal representatives and NGOs, resulting in official recognition of UA and its inclusion in the city's Strategic Land Use Plan. As well, there are municipal laws regulating access to land and provision in the municipal budget for financial support of a UA program.

Waste, water, and environment

Farming on contaminated soil, irrigating with untreated wastewater, and use of chemicals are just some of the environmental and health issues that must be carefully considered in any program to promote food production in urban areas. But on the positive side of the ledger, UA has the potential to contribute to a healthier environment by recycling and reusing some of the city's organic wastes, discouraging practices such as unregulated dumping of garbage, and building on unsuitable land.

A city is a huge nutrient sink, continually absorbing food to feed the ever-growing urban population. Most of the inflow comes from distant locations, and some of it is wasted or deteriorates during transportation or storage. The sink could be made more effective if it recycled more of what it discharges. This might even reduce the need for imports. The sink would be a better place to live — with less air, water, and soil-borne pollution — if it reused some of its wastes. Yet, the lack of effective waste disposal in most cities in the developing world results in huge accumulations of nutrient-rich garbage that threatens the environment and people's health. Finding a safe and economical way to recycle some or all of the municipal and agroindustrial waste holds the promise of a "triple win": clean up the urban environment, reduce the threat to health, and increase agriculture production by replacing soil nutrients.

In West Africa, CFP and its sibling, IDRC's People, Land, and Water (PLAW) program, partnered with the International Water Management Institute (IWMI) in a research project to determine if urban waste composting really does offer a win–win situation for urban and peri-urban farmers and municipalities. The research team, including staff and students from several Ghanaian universities, studied three cities in Ghana: Accra, Kumasi, and Tamale.

The team looked at the supply side of organic waste, the demand for compost, processing options, the economics of composting and alternatives, as well as the institutional and legal aspects. They found that UA, combined with landscaping and other uses, could absorb as much as 20% of the available organic waste. (A similar finding was reached a few years earlier by researchers in the city of Santiago de los Caballeros in the Dominican Republic, which has since launched a community composting program.) Subsidies would be needed for waste management and composting, but the costs could be offset somewhat by sales of compost and the reduction in the amount of waste.

The researchers envisioned a citywide system for recycling as much of the solid organic waste as possible, producing several types of compost to cater to a mixed clientele. This would range from numerous small community-based units supplying nearby farming households with high-quality compost for food production, to large processing plants producing truckloads for enterprises requiring large volumes of lesser quality products for purposes such as woodlot amendment, landfilling, and landscaping (Dreschel et al. 2004).

Closing the nutrient loop

The highly intensive nature of most UA and the limited land base on which it is practiced results in rapid loss of soil fertility. But many urban farmers also keep livestock, particularly in peri-urban areas, sometimes for the main purpose of fertilizing their crop fields. IDRC supported a six-city project located in Senegal and the Gambia to "close the nutrient loop." The researchers aimed to develop integrated horticulture–livestock systems that would increase productivity and improve the livelihoods of urban farmers (Fall and Fall 2001).

The project also evaluated the effectiveness of incorporating some agricultural by-products into livestock feeding systems. The result was to add value to waste products and improve long-term productivity on relatively small areas of agricultural land in urban and peri-urban areas. Livestock farming in the six cities studied also raises particularly tricky issues for urban planners — cattle and traffic do not mix well — and the research emphasized the need for the planners to work with the producers to better integrate livestock into the urban mix (Akinbamijo and Fall 2002).

This project in the Gambia and Senegal not only increased incomes and improved land use, it also had major impacts on the city environment. As part of the project, the use of chemicals and pesticides was closely monitored, and farmers were encouraged to make full use of waste products from both horticulture and livestock production as alternatives to chemical fertilizers. Both the public and the authorities were made aware of the health dangers associated with careless use of toxic chemicals.

Mapping waste supply and demand

Solid waste management and UA were also the subject of an IDRC-supported project in the city of Santiago de los Caballeros in the Dominican Republic. This was the first CFP project to focus on the link between UA and waste management. It was also the first IDRC-supported project to generate a geographic information system (GIS) map of the distribution of UA cultivation at the city block level over an entire city (del Rosario et al. 1999).

With a rapidly growing population of more than 400 000, the city was facing a deteriorating physical environment as a result of inadequate waste management. The local university-based Centro de Estudios Urbanos y Regionales (CEUR) and the municipality of Santiago had a long-standing cooperation agreement. Building on this institutional set-up IDRC supported a project to explore ways in which UA could assist the city to make better use of local resources to improve the living environment as well as to provide inexpensive food for the urban poor.

At the outset, the city was able to handle only about one-third of the waste it produced. There were many neighbourhoods with no connection to the sewer system, and local industries were discharging toxic waste into the Yaque River, the main water source for the city and for crop irrigation. Maps produced by the project team showed the location of unauthorized garbage dumps and areas of off-plot cultivation (vacant land that is not designated for agricultural or horticultural use) combined in Figure 2. These

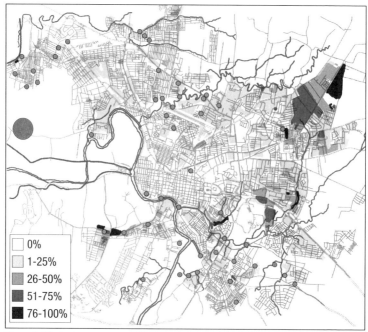

Figure 2. Waste dumps (●) and off-plot cultivation (shaded areas) in Santiago de los Caballeros.

maps showed where volumes of organic wastes potentially could be used in nearby agricultural activities — supply and demand in close proximity resulting in cost savings.

The project team used the results of their research to assist in producing an official plan for the integrated management of solid wastes, the creation of a commission, and the implementation of a pilot project on community-based waste management (PUCMM 1998). This pilot project not only reduced the amount of solid waste to be disposed of, it also supplied fresh, affordable food to the urban poor and provided some additional income. After the project was completed, the city created a Municipal Program on Urban Agriculture to support organic waste recycling and poverty alleviation.

Reducing waste, feeding the poor

The goals were similar in an IDRC-supported project in Haiti, which also received CIDA support. However, the political and policy context was in marked contrast to that found in most other LAC cities where IDRC had worked. The country's highly centralized governmental structure was in crisis at the time of the project in the late 1990s. Many major donors had suspended their aid, except for a few humanitarian organizations such as CARE-Haiti, which is involved in numerous small-scale agricultural and health projects in the country.

The city government of the capital, Port-au-Prince, was functioning very precariously and government involvement in the project had to be sought at the ward level, with city councillors approving and promoting fieldwork in their own constituencies. Although in this way the project could expect to generate little impact on public policy, it could do much through working with local community organizations and NGOs.

Three-quarters of the 1.2 million citizens of Port-au-Prince live in severe poverty in slums known as *bidonvilles*. Regular employment is scarce: fewer than one person in five of working age earns a salary. Not surprisingly, many households have a difficult time meeting their basic food requirements. Malnutrition and anemia are common among children and lactating mothers. If food is a "basic luxury" anywhere, it is here!

Waste production is very high in the densely populated *bidonvilles* but it is estimated to contain as much as 80% organic matter, with the potential to provide an excellent growth medium for vegetables if turned into compost. In most areas, household waste simply piles up around the houses, in ravines, and in other open spaces creating a health hazard. The project aimed to find ways of composting some of the waste — particularly kitchen waste and other organic material — for use in intensive gardens. Intensive because housing density leaves little open space. Working closely with a national NGO, Gardens of Haiti, community-based organizations, and the ward councillors, as well as the Ministries of the Environment and Agriculture, the researchers at CARE-Haiti developed simple technologies and container growing techniques that began to show results in a matter of months.

People quickly adapted the techniques, improvising many different kinds of containers, including old kitchen pots, baskets, used tires, even old television and radio frames — demonstrating that even nonorganic waste can have its uses in UA. In addition to composted organic waste, some cattle and horse manure was used. Some participants simply lined containers with household waste rather than composting it. Midway through the project, gardens also began to appear on buildings with solid rooftops, a largely unused space until then. Many owners shared their roofs with neighbours, thus creating "neighbourhood rooftop gardens." Crops included staples such as carrots, beets, and tomatoes, as well as fast-growing leafy vegetables such as spinach and Swiss chard.

The project rapidly grew well beyond its original scale. Fourteen demonstration gardens were set up initially, and some 1 100 people (more than half of them women) in 68 groups were trained to set up and operate gardens. Local organizations were trained in the creation of small businesses. The number of participating wards grew from 2 in 1996 to 16 by 1999, with 3 more joining in the city of Gonaïves, for a total of 19 instead of the 3 originally planned (Regis et al. 2000). The approach not only improved families' diet and health, it also created social bonds in communities, strengthened women's roles, reduced expenditures, and caused a change of attitude toward waste management. Now, instead of being able to afford vegetables from the markets only once or twice a week, fresh, tasty produce was available daily. Many participants attributed the improved health of their children — evidenced by fewer medical visits and better performance at school — to their daily consumption of fresh vegetables.

On the Web
THE RESEARCH

Managing municipal wastewater

In 1990, the World Bank estimated that in the LAC region alone half-a-million hectares of agricultural crops were being irrigated with urban wastewater, most of which was untreated. A much larger area was being irrigated with surface water that was contaminated with untreated wastewater.

Between 1977 and 1989, IDRC pioneered two projects with the Pan American Center for Sanitary Engineering and Environmental Sciences (CEPIS). The first studied the treatment efficiency of an experimental multiple-lagoon system in the municipality of San Juan, in Lima, Peru. The researchers documented the system's high efficiency in removing parasites, viruses, and pathogenic bacteria. A model used to estimate the water retention time required in the lagoons for removal of these elements proved to be a very useful tool to design and operate similar systems elsewhere. The second project enabled CEPIS to define a reliable methodology to assess the sanitary quality of agricultural products irrigated with wastewater, and the results were key components of a regional training strategy.

Since then, cities in Argentina, Chile, Mexico, and Peru have adopted these methods. But after more than a decade of replicating the system, CEPIS noted problems with several of the plants and approached IDRC for help in improving existing systems and the design of new ones. Between 2000 and 2002, the project identified, documented, and analyzed different types of existing domestic wastewater management systems in 13 countries of the region. It found that although wastewater is widely used for irrigation, reuse is the aspect that receives the least attention.

The researchers assessed 20 different management systems — with and without treatment, with and without reuse. The project's technical committee then developed a more comprehensive sequence of steps, which are presented in the *Guidelines for the Formulation of Projects*, probably the single most important output of this project. In these guidelines, CEPIS recast its own approach in a new light, tapping into the insights gained from the case studies. The guidelines provide much needed advice on critical issues of wastewater management, for which legislation in the region is either inadequate or nonexistent (CEPIS 2002). A more recent IDRC project has assisted CEPIS to validate these *Guidelines* with their target public (see http://www.bvsde.ops-oms.org/bvsaar/e/proyecto/guiaproyeng.pdf).

Reducing the pollution load

West Africa is also urbanizing rapidly; here too fresh water is an increasingly precious commodity in cities. Since 1990, IDRC has supported a team of researchers led by the Institut fondamental d'Afrique noire (IFAN) at the Cheikh Anta Diop University of Dakar, Senegal. A series of projects is developing locally appropriate systems for the integrated management, treatment, and agricultural reuse of domestic wastewater.

Urban and peri-urban vegetable farming contributes most of the fresh produce consumed by the city, and the concern was that most of these crops were irrigated with untreated, nutrient-loaded wastewater. This produced higher yields, but raised questions about health issues. By then, Dakar had already suffered cholera epidemics attributed to the consumption of vegetables irrigated with inadequate wastewater. In almost all water-treatment processes tested, pollution loads were reduced, but none reduced bacteria enough to meet norms for unrestricted agriculture or pisciculture. The project recommended a combination of different processes to reach such norms and much of the researchers' subsequent work was devoted to testing such a system (Niang 1996).

In mid-1992, the lead researcher, Seydou Niang, suggested to a national governmental commission on the environment, that future treatment plants should not be copies of imported models but rather take into account the country's own socioeconomic peculiarities. He was subsequently asked by the Ministry of Science and Technology to prepare a report on the state of the art of wastewater-treatment technologies in the country.

Meanwhile, back on the streets of Dakar, a national development NGO called Environnement et développement du Tiers Monde (ENDA) had started to work with communities within the city to install more affordable collective small-diameter sewerage systems. In 1998, they approached the IFAN team to validate and fine-tune the treatment and reuse component of two community-scale schemes, built in Castor and Diokoul with funding from the Canadian International Development Agency (CIDA). The ENDA system was cost-effective, with a high rate of investment recovery and ENDA was lobbying public utilities to take up more appropriate waste-management strategies.

By 1998 the policy environment, both at the state and municipal levels, was evolving positively. The national sanitation agency (Office national de l'assainissement du Sénégal, ONAS) had

On the Web
THE RESEARCH

become more interested in these systems. A collaborative agreement was struck between ENDA, IFAN, and ONAS during a networking workshop sponsored by IDRC in Ouagadougou, Burkina Faso. A pilot project would test two aquatic treatment systems, one using water lettuce in Castor and the other using bulrushes along with tilapia fish in Diokoul. The project, also funded by CIDA, showed that natural treatment plants are clearly more robust than mechanical systems (Niang and Gaye 2002). A new project will focus on bringing the existing systems in line with WHO guidelines (Faruqui et al. 2004).

Growing gardens with greywater

In Jordan, one of the most water-scarce countries in the world, the shortage of water creates a double threat for the poor: food and water insecurity. Almost three-quarters of Jordan's population lives in cities and towns, and in these urban centres there is barely enough water to drink, let alone enough for agriculture. It is estimated that the amount of water available to each individual is less than 200 cubic metres per year. Below 1 000 cubic metres, water scarcity can impede economic development and harm human health.

Greywater is water that has been used for domestic purposes such as bathing or laundry. The potential to reuse this water for UA was the objective of a project jointly funded by IDRC and the Inter-Islamic Network on Water Resources and Development and Management (INWRDAM) in Jordan. The project took a new approach to food insecurity and water scarcity in the region, exploring water management techniques, simple technological innovations, and creative agricultural practices.

An initial survey by the Department of Statistics estimated that households in the city of Amman tend to over 50 000 home gardens, totaling 648 hectares, although only 25% of available space was under cultivation. Most of these gardens were irrigated with fresh water from the public distribution system. At the same time, nearly one-third of all households suffered from water scarcity, and many complained of the high price of water. Some households, however, were already using water-saving practices such as collecting rainwater and applying greywater directly to their gardens (Shakhatreh and Raddad 2000).

Dr Murad Jabay Bino, executive director of INWRDAM, stresses the importance of finding ways to conserve and reuse water. He adds that reusing water for irrigation is a new area of research for UA that has substantially reduced the demand for freshwater. He believes that the techniques for wastewater reuse developed in this project can help produce more food for the poor. But he warns that it is essential to ensure that reusing wastewater is both safe and socially acceptable.

On the Web
THE RESEARCH

The researchers met these requirements in tests in a small town south of Amman. They developed a wastewater-recycling system that allows water from household uses to be reused in home gardens. Involving some minor modifications to household plumbing, the system diverts water from kitchen and bathroom sinks through a filter instead of allowing it to go down the drain. The project has exceeded expectations. Initial water savings are estimated to be at least 15%, and households are using the recycled water to increase crops such as eggplants, herbs, and olives. The use of greywater in market gardens is reported to have increased household incomes by anywhere from 10% to 40% (Bino et al. 2003).

The Ministry of Planning was so impressed with these results that it supported the construction of a further 700 systems across the country based on the INWRDAM model. As a bonus, the new technology has created a thriving local business enterprise involving engineers, plumbers, and contractors. Other Middle East countries are also showing interest, and INWRDAM is developing a network of partners throughout the region to share knowledge and research. For its part, IDRC is supporting similar projects in Lebanon and the West Bank and Gaza, researching policies for UA and wastewater reuse.

Food security and incomes

Food security has been defined by the World Bank (1986) as "access by all people at all times to enough food for an active healthy life." For the urban poor, food security decreases in relation to the portion of the household budget that must be spent on purchasing food. As witnessed in the *bidonvilles* of Haiti, when that budget no longer stretches to provide enough food, coping strategies are few. In some cases, desperate people resort to scavenging garbage dumps for leftover food and rotting fruits and vegetables to feed their families. Seen in this light, UA is a welcome and perhaps even an inevitable alternative.

Haiti may be the poorest nation in the Western hemisphere, but it is by no means the only country where poverty threatens people's food security. The seaport of Fortaleza in Brazil is the capital of the state of Ceará, but it has fallen on hard times. Unemployment is widespread, an estimated 70% of families earn monthly incomes of less than (US) $150, and hunger is rampant. It was in this environment that CFP undertook two projects. The first was a study of past and current efforts to promote UA, including a cooperative program funded by the state government and the European Union (EU) to promote backyard and community gardening, small animal husbandry, and fruit-tree planting for economic, health, and microclimatic benefits.

Based on the lessons and recommendations from the first EU project, IDRC supported a second, more ambitious program that included a series of pilot projects. These projects were located in peri-urban regions and included aquaculture in cages, vegetables, fruit trees, medicinal gardens, and production of herbal remedies (Albuquerque 1996a,b,c). Working closely with NGOs and community organizations, the project team conducted numerous workshops with the local people. They developed training programs through courses and seminars and organized exchanges with technicians and students from other institutions, both local and from other countries. The project team also produced books, videos, and other training materials (Albuquerque 1999). All results of the pilot projects were submitted to the state government to be made available for other researchers in the field of UA (Cabannes 1997).

Both the fish farming and the fruit, vegetable, and herb gardening involved many young people. The project provided training under the National Rural Apprenticeship Service (SENAR) and offered work opportunities. Training included production techniques, composting, planting and care of fruit trees, soil improvement, irrigation, and fertilization. A community medicine garden was established by women in the project. They received training in plant production, drying, home processing, and handling. A pharmacist was employed to explain the production of medicinal plants providing alternative medicines for common illnesses such as colds and flu, bronchitis, asthma, diarrhea, mycosis, and some intestinal parasites (Collombon et al. 1996).

The end result was great demand in the communities for more such projects. One group managed to raise enough money to start their own laboratory for medicinal plants, as well as a therapeutic massage centre. Others used the knowledge gained during the project to develop more aquaculture sites, and even children were being trained to build fish cages.

Lessons learned

In Part 4 we will examine the lessons offered by the experience in these and scores of other projects supported by IDRC and our partners, and how these lessons can be applied.

Learning from Experience

Urban agriculture is a means of securing incomes, and therefore has an important role in urban planning. Urban agriculture also converts idle laying land into green space, and green zones and greenbelts are important for the city authorities.
Daniel Sackey, Directorate for Food and Agriculture, Accra, Ghana

The previous chapter provides a cross-section of some of the UA projects supported by IDRC over more than two decades. This chapter draws some lessons from that unique volume of practical experience, particularly as it pertains to the interaction between development research and policy interventions, whether through site-specific projects or broader institutional programs.

A great deal has been learned over the past two decades through support for close to 100 projects in 40 countries. There is no question that what was once seen as a novel area for research has now become mainstream. The continuing growth of cities, particularly in developing countries, is nothing short of phenomenal and is likely to continue for the foreseeable future. The issues that are raised by this avalanche of urbanization can no longer be ignored. The situation demands innovative approaches and new ways of thinking — the city planners of past generations simply did not conceive of cities on the scale that now exists. The old paradigms of city and country, urban and rural, city folk and farmers, no longer apply.

Cities can never become completely self-sustaining but, as we have seen, they can become greener, cleaner, healthier, and more sustainable. And they must — the alternative is unimaginable chaos and unthinkable squalor. Urban agriculture is not the total solution to the issues facing the future of cities in developing countries, but it is an essential part of any program to make those cities more livable, and to improve the lives of the city dwellers. And research is key to realizing the full potential of UA. The next few pages offer some practical lessons for city planners, politicians, policymakers, and urban farmers based on what has been learned through pioneering IDRC-supported research in the field.

Land and space

Land — who owns it, who can use it, how safe is it, how secure? These are key questions both for the practitioners of UA and for the policymakers and planners. But there is another key question that cities need to be able to answer if they are to take full advantage of the benefits offered by UA: **How much land is there really, and where is it?** Analysis of open space areas within cities in Africa and Latin America clearly shows that in most cities there is far more land available than is generally recognized by city managers and elected officials. There are vacant lots, public lands around buildings such as schools and hospitals, undeveloped or abandoned sites, and so on. Perhaps the first lesson, then, is the importance of taking stock — creating an inventory of *all* the land in the city that could be used for some form of production, whether permanently or temporarily, as was done in Dar es Salaam and Kampala, Governador Valadares and Santiago de los Caballeros.

Maps of urban Harare (Figure 3) show that cultivated open space doubled from 8% in 1990 to nearly 17% in 1994. Areas close to industrial districts shrank, while others expanded: next to high-density, low-income residential districts, along roadways and waterways, in the central business district, and in parkland and upscale neighbourhoods. But these maps only show part of the picture. Much of the cultivated open space extending beyond the official city boundary was not recorded. Neither were open fields left in fallow nor cropping and livestock on residential and other lots, built or not. The lesson: you need to know what you are looking for when designing a UA survey.

Establishing what lands are available for UA is an important first step. However, **not all vacant land is suitable for food production**. Studies in Latin American cities have shown that suitability depends on your "toolkit" of systems technologies, how diverse it is, and the options you have on hand. Ingenuity can find ways to effectively "recycle" derelict industrial sites. For example, in Cuba and in Argentina, producers were faced with the challenge of contaminated soil in some areas. They overcame the problem by building raised beds filled with soil and compost that was trucked in.

Another option demonstrated successfully in several cities in both Africa and Latin America has been to use "unsuitable" sites to cultivate flowers instead of food — floriculture instead of horti-culture. Sale of the flowers, often for export, provides the income families need to purchase food.

Establishing how land is available and determining the suitability of that land for various types of production are essential first

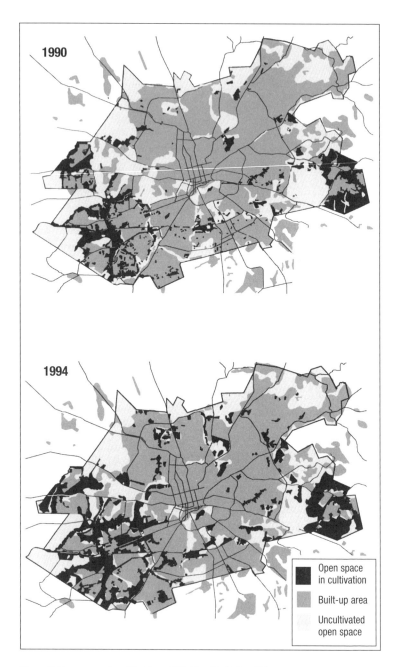

1990

1994

Open space
in cultivation

Built-up area

Uncultivated
open space

Figure 3. Open space in cultivation within the city limits of Harare, 1990 and 1994.

steps to developing a healthy agriculture within the cities of the developing world. However, the research also points clearly to the fact that, for many would-be city farmers, **access to land is more of a constraint than is its availability**. This is particularly true for the poor, and especially for women. Ensuring access to that land on a fair and equitable basis can be difficult, and one of the keys to ensuring fairness is to encourage the producer to form organizations. Clear and well-publicized regulations for the use of land have also been shown to make life more predictable for city farmers.

Predictability is important. People are unlikely to invest time and scarce resources into UA if they are afraid that they will be evicted from the land before their crop is ready for harvest or that the crop will be destroyed by over-zealous officials. Which points to another lesson, a corollary to the previous one: **security of tenure is more important than ownership**. In fact, it is clear that insisting on ownership as a prerequisite for UA artificially creates a scarcity of land.

Research has demonstrated that there are many ways to provide security of tenure. For example, NGOs or church groups can help by negotiating leases with city officials. Such agreements should be made in writing because this increases the producers' perception of security. Where the producers are organized, it is far easier to reach leasing agreements. There is also a need to be flexible, to allow production systems to evolve over time, to use space when it is available, and to eventually relocate to other sites in the city when it is appropriate. An example would be to allow the use of a vacant building site until construction is scheduled, under the mutual and formal agreement that the producers are committed to move to another undeveloped site, ideally with some assistance, when the need to evacuate arises.

Although we are considering here issues that relate to land, we should also consider the lesson that **in the city, space may be more critical than land itself.** Certainly land is important, but a great deal of production can (and does) take place in many cities where no additional land is needed. Space, after all, is three-dimensional and space embraces the built-up area as much as the unbuilt area. Space in this context encompasses rooftops, walls, fences, sheds, shelves, basements, ponds, and even window boxes. There are production systems designed for all environments — indoor and outdoor.

In Haiti, for example, concrete rooftops become fertile "ground" to produce fresh vegetables grown in a wide variety of containers. Built-up areas in general tend to be less exploited, but there is great potential even in the most densely developed areas of the city. People are often seen to grow crops or keep livestock within the walls of their unfinished, still roofless house. Mushrooms can be grown in trays indoors. Various species of fish can be raised in tanks or artificial ponds. Small livestock such as guinea pigs in cages require little space and water, and are inexpensive to feed. They are a significant source of meat in some central Andean cities. Silkworms can be a valuable source of income. Medicinal herbs can be cultivated in containers and processed in the home. The list goes on.

There is such a variety of scale and types of productions systems that the opportunity of fitting UA with particular urban uses and at particular moments in time seems unlimited. However, many of these practices contravene various regulations for the use of urban dwellings, and this has implications for the revision of building codes and regulations to remove restrictions that may be more apparent than real. If city planners and administrators learn to "think outside of the box," then the range of options really opens up (Premat 2003).

It is not only the city planners, however, who need to discover new ways of thinking about agriculture in the cities. Consider that extension workers are invariably trained in rural areas, not in the cities, and thus naturally tend to follow norms and standards that are intended for the rural agriculture and may have little relevance in the urban environment. **To assess the agricultural potential of a site, you need to have a multidisciplinary approach** — providing an all-encompassing view that involves architects and planners as well as agronomists and the producers themselves.

Some major challenges for research on land-related issues remain. These include the need to adapt some of the more profitable UA systems so that they can be used by people who currently lack the money, resources, or the know-how to take advantage of opportunities to increase family incomes. Equally important is the need to help poor urban farmers get organized so that they can better negotiate with wealthy landowners and municipal governments. Civil society groups and NGOs have demonstrated their effectiveness in helping with this aspect of the issue.

Waste disposal and health

Cities everywhere produce a lot of waste, and the waste load of most cities in developing countries is largely organic. Agriculture, particularly **urban agriculture, represents a principal market for the productive use of much of this organic material,** if only because the cities don't have many other options. There are very few other industries that can make use of large amounts of organic waste — biogas production being one possibility that is still largely in the experimental stage. Urban farmers however are ideal reusers of waste close to the source points.

That being said, it is true that UA cannot make use of all of the waste that a large city produces. But, to maximize productive use of organic, composted waste, it is important that waste-treatment centres be close to the areas where UA is going on, as the projects in Ghana and Brazil demonstrate. The proximity of a waste-treatment centre makes it more attractive for producers to use the material by reducing transportation costs. Recycling organic waste products is particularly important for cities in arid environments, such as much of sub-Saharan Africa.

The valuable lesson here is that organic waste management should include various systems of collection and treatment. **The integrated approach to solid waste management should include a variety of products for a variety of users.** For example, there might be compost bins at the city block level, larger-scale treatment centres at the district level, and so on. Several different kinds of compost and mulches may be produced to meet different needs. High-grade compost, which sells at a relatively high price, may be economically moved and sold within a wide territory. Transportation costs dictate that lower grade (and lower priced) products be sold close to home. This emphasizes yet again the value of producers forming organized groups that can share the costs of bulk transportation. On the other hand, low-quality, less expensive products, such as coarse mulch used for landscaping and similar projects, could be sold by the truckload to contractors.

Public education is an important component for the successful introduction of recycling programs. Incentives are needed to encourage people to recycle. This applies to both the producers and the consumers of organic waste. Such public education should include the importance of separating different kinds of waste materials and for the producers the use of safe water and the minimum use of pesticides.

It can be difficult to persuade producers to "go organic" because the intensive systems of agriculture that are common in UA demand the use of chemical fertilizers. One solution to this issue is to demonstrate the law of diminishing returns — where you have to use more and more inputs, both fertilizers and pesticides, to produce the same amount of product.

So far we have been discussing solid wastes. What about wastewater? This is a resource that is virtually ignored by all except for the urban farmers. UA will continue to use whatever water is available regardless of the source, so it is very important to do something about this. **Not doing anything about the use of wastewater will only increase the vulnerability to epidemics of disease.** By the same token, not paying attention to the issue is not going to solve your problem, whether you are a public health official, a water resource manager, or a politician.

As with solid wastes, different qualities of wastewater can be used safely for the production of different agricultural goods. Similarly, separation at source and utilization close to source are keys to optimal use, with minimal treatment and distribution costs.

Technologies do exist to treat different types of wastewater at different scales and to produce end products of different qualities. For example, the greywater project in Jordan reused household wastewater at the site; in Fortaleza, wastewater was piped to a common plot of land where it was used to irrigate an orchard. On a larger scale, the CEPIS systems in Peru provide water from settling ponds that is used by thousands of people. The CEPIS project also safely uses water from the final stage of cleaning for aquaculture production. And on the outskirts of Dakar, Senegal, two community-scale wastewater schemes demonstrated water-treatment systems that are both effective and affordable.

Such systems are more effective in developing countries than the large-scale, centralized, capital-intensive systems that were developed for the industrialized North and simply don't work in many developing contexts. These and other IDRC-supported research projects have shown that the health risks currently caused by the use of wastewater that is untreated or insufficiently treated in urban or peri-urban agriculture can be overcome by simple measures. These measures include modifying irrigation practices — for example, irrigating the base of the plant instead of watering the leaves or using underground watering systems — and matching the choice of crops or products to the quality of the water used — for example, using poor quality water on flowers or foods that must be cooked before eating. Equally important are the post-harvest handling of products and the working conditions of people in contact with wastewater in the fields.

The key lesson here is that **because the use of untreated waste-water is growing so fast, more has to be done to protect both producers and consumers**. Public education on the risks of working with untreated wastewater is important, as are agri-culture extension and financial assistance. Market incentives for the producers to use safer wastewater for irrigation have also been shown to be effective. And, once again, the advantage of producers working together in groups is demonstrated, enabling them to gain access to technologies that they would otherwise be unable to afford.

Once again too, there are implications at the building code level. Having systems built into homes that can recycle greywater, as demonstrated in Jordan, can alleviate water shortages, improve diets, and increase family incomes. Such systems are particularly applicable to cities in arid regions.

The research challenges remaining in the area of wastewater treatment and health include the need for cost–benefit analysis of wastewater-treatment systems for agricultural use at different scales. Studies have shown that the more expensive fresh water is — the more people have to pay for water — the more they are willing to conserve and recycle water. There is also a need to study possible forms of legislation that can be used to reduce the health risks related to the use of wastewater.

Food and nutrition

Food supply crises in the developing world can come about as a result of a number of factors: political instability, climate change, market globalization, and so on. Whatever the cause, a crisis in food supply tends to affect people in urban areas more than in rural areas, and **women and children are particularly vulnerable when food is in short supply**.

Studies in Africa and Latin America have shown that food expenditures are already **the** major item for most poor families even when there is not a shortage of food. Many must spend up to 80% of their income on this "basic luxury" and, for some, one meal a day is the norm. For such families, and even for many middle-income families, imported foods are simply out of reach and so offer no relief. In any case, countries that are the worst hit by food shortages are typically also the ones that can least afford to rely on external food sources to make up the shortfall. Here, more than anywhere else, UA is a critical supplier of certain types of foods that tend to be rich in micronutrients, such as fresh greens and vegetables.

Thus, self-provisioning — growing even a small amount of food for home consumption — is a very important strategy for many poor and middle-income households. Evidence suggests that children in these households show better health than children who do not have access to self-provisioned food. In the *bidonvilles* of Haiti, for example, parents say that children who now regularly eat fresh vegetables from their container gardens do better in school. And there is an additional benefit: with the money saved, families are able to buy other food items that they could not otherwise afford.

Many of those engaged in UA are not doing it just for self-provisioning. Although UA is a main occupation for only a minority of those who farm in the cities, it is a very important second or even third occupation for many people. In every city where IDRC has supported research, it is clear that a very large number of people spend some part of their time working at UA. Growing and processing food in cities creates a lot of employment, many thousands of part-time and full-time jobs, and has the potential to create many more. For many families it helps to reduce the economic uncertainty that comes with unemployment and employment instability, meaning there will always be food on the table.

There are some interesting side effects to the increasing practice of UA. One is that the urban food supply tends at the city level to depress the seasonal variations in food prices somewhat. It also increases the availability of particular types of food across the seasons. In this way, UA production tends to regularize the supply of fresh produce at affordable prices. Another — though not strictly scientific — is that it helps the self-esteem of the people who are engaged in it. Nothing is more depressing than being unable to provide for yourself and your family.

Many challenges remain in the rapid development of UA and its relationship with food security. Members of the RUAF network, for example, are now looking into how and when urban agriculture can best be made part of urban food-security strategies. How should different production systems be combined to optimize nutritional returns to practicing households and beyond? How can we quantify the contribution of UA to the food status of a city or a country? How can we determine when and how UA makes a critical difference? Not so long ago seeking answers to these questions would have seemed academic at best. But today, as the majority of people on this planet (and mainly in the developing world) coalesce into agglomerations of a size and scale never seen before, finding answers is politically desirable and no acceptable means of bringing food security to all should be discarded.

While further research would undoubtedly shed light on these questions, it is nevertheless clear from the examples in this book that city officials who have supported, if not fully embraced UA, have reaped considerable benefit. Sharing the fruits of that collective experience is the subject of the next chapter.

Part 5

Recommendations

On the Web
THE LESSONS

Our urban agriculture activities promote production, increase competition, improve the quality of products, and allow us to identify discrepancies between local supply and demand, enabling us to consolidate processing and marketing. Our regulations accurately reflect our view that small producers and vendors, men and women, are important actors.
Mayor Washington Ipenza, Villa Maria del Triunfo, Lima, Peru

As stated at the beginning this book, urban agriculture is here to stay. Accepting that, the question then becomes how to manage it. There is ample evidence that attempting to suppress "unauthorized" agricultural activity in cities has little effect other than to make the lives of the urban poor even more precarious. There is also evidence that UA has the potential to make many positive contributions to the life of the city — from alleviating hunger and improving child nutrition, to providing employment and income, and even to helping clean up the urban environment. Little wonder then that many governments, at all levels, have opted to develop policies that integrate UA into the urban framework.

This chapter offers some recommendations for governments that have made the decision to work with UA rather than against it.

These recommendations may also prove useful to researchers, NGOs, community activists, and others involved in the study or practice of UA. They are based on IDRC's two decades of accumulated research experience in the field and draw on some of the lessons outlined in the previous chapter as well as on personal experience.

1. Municipal governments should start with the right question: What can UA do for my city (not what can my city do for it)?

If you dig deeply and widely enough, you may be surprised by what you will find. From composting, to environmental risk management and community gardens, local governments often support or manage far more "urban agriculture" activities than they realize. In Vancouver, for example, many municipal departments are responsible for UA-type activities (Table 2). The real potential, however, lies in making better connections between these activities, as in Havana, Rosario, Cuenca, Cagayan de Oro, and Vancouver. Governments that have developed, or are developing, UA policies have done so because they view it as a tool to address multiple challenges faced by the city, its environment, its economy, and its people. The best examples draw on a wide range of actors — municipal staff, nongovernmental organizations (NGOs), community-based organizations (CBOs), organized producers, food processors, and traders — to develop robust policies to address everything from waste management, to employment, and public health (IAGU 2002; UMP-LAC/UN-HABITAT and IPES 2003).

An inclusive approach to municipal programing tends to make public policy more comprehensive, durable, and consistent. It also reduces the all too familiar pitfall whereby the outcomes of successful projects remain localized or are short-lived. As Quito's Director of Planning, Diego Carrion, clearly stated following his involvement in an IDRC-supported project in his city, "we are not so much interested in the success of the [local] Panecillo project itself as we are in a strategy that will allow us to replicate similar

Table 2. Municipal departments responsible for UA-type activities in the city of Vancouver, Canada.

City initiative	Municipal department
City Farmer garden (compost demonstration and water conservation site)	Engineering Services Solid Waste Management
Composting (city, home, apartment, backyard, and worm) and compost information hotline	Engineering Services Solid Waste Management Planning (Central Area)
Green streets program	Engineering Services Streets, Structures, and Greenways Planning (Central Area)
Neighbourhood and city greenways	Engineering Services Streets, Structures, and Greenways
Natural yard care	Engineering Services Solid Waste Management
Environmental grants	Financial Services
Greenhouse gas reduction	Office of Sustainability
Community gardens	Parks Board Real Estate Planning (Central Area) Engineering Services
Farmers' markets	Parks Board
Fruit and nut trees	Parks Board Planning and Operations Planning (Central Area)
Green building strategy	Planning (Central Area)
Childcare grants (includes food supplement program, etc.)	Social Planning
Aboriginal initiatives (UBC Farm Community Kitchen Garden)	Social Planning
Social sustainability initiatives (farmers' markets, community gardens, edible landscaping, etc.)	Social Planning
Food system assessment	Social Planning
Food policy staff team	Social Planning

Source: City of Vancouver, 2005.

Note: Many of the initiatives listed in this table predate Vancouver's official food policy mandate and take place under the auspices of departments with little or no involvement by the food policy staff team. For more information on Vancouver's Food Policy Council, see www.city.vancouver.bc.ca/commsvcs/socialplanning/initiatives/foodpolicy/council.htm.

On the Web
THE LESSONS

projects throughout the metropolitan area." Quito has since created a municipal program of UA.

Regardless of how well food production and processing is integrated into the urban fabric, policymakers should ensure that policies aimed at urban and peri-urban agriculture complement others directed at rural agriculture. While this usually requires input from other levels of government, it allows authorities to capitalize on the comparative advantages of urban and rural agriculture to help ensure the food security for all citizens, regardless of where they live.

2. Use UA to make suitable vacant space productive for all

Municipal governments that have mapped their city's open spaces are amazed by how much space sits idle at any given time. There is usually much more happening in your city than meets the eye, even a bird's eye. Unused urban space is a wasted opportunity — an asset denied to a community's well-being and a brake on the city's development.

Municipal governments urgently need to develop and use tools that will answer a number of questions:

➤ How much space in their city is unused, underused, or misused? Where? How much of this could be made more attractive, more productive, and more profitable in social, economic, and environmental terms? How much could be achieved, in the short or longer term, through UA?

➤ How much space is actually being used by urban producers? What kind of spaces and what types of production systems are they using? What are the benefits and constraints? Is more space required? Where?

➤ What production systems are best suited for particular land uses and particular sites? What infrastructure and facilities exist —

functional or not — that have room for or could be revamped to support production, storage, processing, marketing, or recycling activities, as was done in Dar es Salaam and Rosario?

Armed with this kind of knowledge, municipalities often can encourage UA for little or no cost. In Quito, Ecuador, for instance, local markets were developed along major transportation arteries. In Santiago de los Caballeros, Dominican Republic, indiscriminate domestic waste dumps became municipal composting sites when they were located near farmers' fields. Governments can also create room for agriculture in all kinds of new developments — residential, commercial, industrial, institutional, recreational, or transportation and utility.

3. Include UA as an urban land-use category and as an economic function in your planning system

UA is a dynamic land use that adjusts quickly to a city's growth and development. But it suffers from an image problem and is seldom recognized as a valid land-use category. To gain the full benefit from UA activities, this must change.

By matching UA production systems with compatible open spaces, areas can be identified where UA is more stable (such as rights-of-way and "unconstructable" areas) as well as areas where it may be more temporary (sites awaiting development, for example). Confined central areas of the city could benefit from more intensive, usually more profitable activities, like mushroom growing, silk-worm culture, or medicinal plant cultivation. Sites exposed to contaminants could be given over to ornamental crops rather than risking potential health risks from growing and marketing vegetables.

Setting aside areas in or around the city for the exclusive and permanent use by UA is unrealistic and self-defeating. For one thing, it ignores the economic reality of land prices in growing cities. More importantly, it misses out on the interactions that UA can have (and should have if it is to prosper) with other urban activities.

4. Use a participatory policy-making approach

The experience of IDRC's partners in Africa and Latin America clearly shows the benefits of using a participatory approach to the development of UA policies. By involving a broad base of stakeholders, municipal authorities are more likely to develop policies that will meet the needs of both the municipality and its constituents, especially the disadvantaged poor (Cissé et al. 2005). Furthermore, more equitable decision-making promotes citizen engagement and buy-in at all levels. As part of any policy development initiative, structures and processes should be developed to identify problems, prioritize actions, and to carry out and monitor interventions.

The municipality should lead a policy-coordinating team representative of the various stakeholders and whose interests cover the breadth of priority issues. Experience has shown that written agreements outlining roles and responsibilities increase the commitments of the various parties involved and increase the chances that the results of the policy process will be adopted.

Where feasible, participants in the policy exercise can use the Internet to communicate among themselves, with other city stakeholders, and with other "resource" cities with similar experiences. For example, cities that simultaneously engage in similar activities can collect and share information (visual, bibliographic, messages, contacts) using a dedicated Web site.

5. Experiment with temporary occupancy permits (TOPs) for urban producers using private and public open spaces

The use of TOPs overcomes a key problem: access to land for the urban poor. TOPs can be granted to groups or individuals, with land lent directly to producers by the landowner or indirectly through the municipal government or an accredited agency.

Regardless of the granting process, TOPs are legally binding documents that should be registered with municipal government to protect land lenders. Doing so provides the stability producers need to invest in more profitable types of products, more productive techniques, and more sustainable site stewardship. It also makes it easier for producers to access technical, financial, marketing, and other services. Finally, it reduces the number of disputes and enables government to relate more directly with land lenders and producers.

The use of TOPs can be encouraged by other policy measures to make the lending of available and suitable space attractive to both public and private landowners. For example, property tax reductions can induce landowners to make unused land or space available. Offering monetary or other incentives to owners of large tracts of vacant space suitable for UA could expand considerably the volume and quality of a city's stock that organized urban producers could access under TOPs arrangements.

6. Support the organization of poor urban producers to manage UA in more and better ways

UA workers and poor producers, in particular, cannot work as effectively as they could if they are not organized and recognized as legitimate. Municipalities have a clear stake in seeing that urban producers are better organized and better represented in local policy processes. By-laws, however well intended, will always be difficult to enforce. It is clear that governments cannot do this job alone, and repression does not work. Municipalities need the collaboration of others, particularly those directly involved in UA production.

IDRC-supported research shows that successful land-seekers tend to belong to a group of some kind. The problem for governments is that most groups to which poor urban producers belong are informal — the poor tend to fall back on customary practices inherited from rural societies and try to adapt these to their urban reality. There is evidence that governments have more to gain than to lose by building on and empowering these types of organizations. However, governments should be aware that many poor urban producers have problems accessing land, even under informal rules. Various groups may be discriminated against or even forbidden from using land on the grounds of class, gender, religion, or ethnic identity. Governments should encourage fair policies to promote the organization of groups and provide equitable access to land for all.

Stable producers' organizations can negotiate terms of tenure to provide greater security for their members. They can represent their members in policy exercises and negotiate contracts with suppliers or buyers on their behalf. They can also strike alliances with other stakeholders with shared interests in urban development strategies. Public and private agencies and NGOs have struck partnerships with producers' organizations to undertake a wide range of activities, including tending public parks, maintaining open spaces, providing security to estates, reforesting areas prone to degradation, discouraging dumping, reducing the costs of wastewater treatment plants, supplying medicine to public health clinics, providing food to schools and government facilities, and even offering local produce in the city's supermarkets.

7. Bring the needed research in tune with your policy exercise at the earliest opportunity

Table 3 focuses on the degree of involvement of governmental institutions in selected IDRC-supported UA research activities. Several recommendations flow from the IDRC experience collected in this table:

→ The objectives and expected results of the research should directly serve the policy exercise it is to support. To go from objectives to results, research and policy steps should alternate

**Table 3. Involvement of government institutions
in selected IDRC-supported projects.**

Location of project	Type of project	Original request	Proposal design	Implemen-tation	Review of results	Use of outputs
Kampala, Uganda	UA-specific study led by academic institution	○	○	◦	◦	●
Harare, Zimbabwe	UA-specific, multistake-holder study to collect baseline data and set priorities led by a national development NGO	○	◦	◦	◦	◦
Dar es Salaam, Tanzania	UA component of broader urban environmental planning exercise led by municipal government and UN agency	●	●	●	●	◦
Quito, Ecuador	UA-specific, multistake-holder city consultation, leading to pilot projects and municipal policy innovations in land use planning, fiscal incentives, microcredit mechanisms, and city budgeting for UA; consultation served as model for other cities	●	●	●	●	●

Note: ○ = no involvement; ◦ = some involvement; ● = significant involvement.

one with another: one policy step guiding the next research step, which in turn will inform a new policy step, and so on.

➤ The policy-leading government agency should be committed to seeing such an interactive process through to completion.

➤ The research must use a methodology that engages government throughout. The ability of a policy-oriented project to engage government and other actors earlier in more stages of the project life leads to more outputs within a shorter period of time.

- ➤ Projects that are led by a government agency and focus specifically on UA are more likely to engage the government into readily using its outputs for progress on UA policy.

- ➤ Projects should use South–South sharing of experiences and expertise. Local processes developed as components of regional projects tend to deliver UA policy results more quickly than those carried out in isolation.

On this final point, municipalities should use their national associations and international federations, as well as international organizations and programs, to share their own experience and obtain information about those of other cities.

Reshaping city life

Knitting UA into the urban fabric begins with recognizing its importance to the lives of local people and to the health of the local environment. By drawing on expertise that exists within their own departments, among resident institutions and engaged citizens, municipal authorities can craft policies to address multiple challenges in a comprehensive and equitable way. As age-old farming and livestock rearing practices adapt to the reality of modern urban life, they will shape a very different future for cities and their citizens.

Part 6

A City of the Future

*We see urban agriculture, including horticulture and forestry, as a
more sustainable way for urban greening. Urban agriculture is the fruit
of good solid waste management and a practical way of improving
urban areas and addressing food supply and distribution.*
Mayor L.S. Duran, Marilao, Philippines

On the Web
THE LESSONS

In this book we have briefly reviewed the progress of urban agriculture in the cities of the South over the past 20 years. Research
projects supported by IDRC and its partners have demonstrated
the benefits of encouraging and supporting food production in
towns and cities instead of attempting to suppress it. We have
considered some of the lessons learned from those projects over
two decades and have presented some recommendations based on
those lessons. Now let's look ahead 20 years.

Imagine for a moment a medium-sized city somewhere in the
South — perhaps in Africa or the Middle East, perhaps in Latin
America or the Caribbean. The city has a population of a little
over one million, an increase of over 50% in the past 20 years,
and still growing. The older parts of the city are densely populated,

but on the outskirts the wealthy have built large suburban homes where once were villages. A river runs through the city, and river-front areas are sometimes flooded during the rainy season. The city has some industry, but the national economy is weak and unemployment or underemployment are common.

Now imagine that this city has been fortunate over the past two decades to be the site of a number of research projects examining various aspects of UA and equally fortunate to have managers and elected officials willing to consider new ideas and make the right decisions. Initially, the city council and its administrators had been cautious about such research. Their traditional approach to UA, which had been deemed illegal, had been periodic attempts to shut it down by arresting or fining producers and destroying their crops. However, this approach had been ineffective — the urban farmers simply moved on to another spot where they could continue to produce a little food. And the results of the research had caused some members of council and city administrators to consider that, given the growing numbers of urban poor and the deteriorating state of the city's environment, perhaps UA was not such a bad thing after all.

Perhaps some of these councillors and administrators had attended a workshop where mayors and councillors from many cities in the region had shared their problems and solutions. No doubt they listened to the experiences of others and absorbed the ideas of the experts, who explained how UA could be used as a tool to strengthen a city's food security, improve the health of the poor, help clean up the environment, and even provide some much needed employment. They took all this to heart and took the message home. Soon their city became part of a regional city network formed to encourage the controlled expansion of UA for all the right reasons.

Fast forward to the year 2025

Another 20 years have passed and we are going to take a tour of our imaginary city to see what the city of the future might look like — a city that has benefited from research, from shared knowledge, and has learned from the experience of other cities as well as from its own policy attempts to integrate UA and its practitioners in urban development. In this city of the future, the way of thinking about urban food security and safety, and the use of space, has changed dramatically. Now UA is anticipated and encouraged rather than opposed or merely tolerated.

First stop on our tour: city hall. A meeting of the Urban Agriculture Committee is underway. The manager of the city's Urban Agriculture Department has just presented a plan to use a portion of all school grounds for gardens that will be planted and maintained by the students, who will share the produce they grow. The matter is controversial only because some are concerned that the gardening activity will interfere with the children's classroom studies. The committee members are well aware that similar schemes in place for some years at several industrial sites and housing developments have been able to produce surprisingly large quantities of fresh produce. The question of balancing the curriculum is referred to the Education Committee, and the plan is approved in principle.

Next stop: the university. The city and the producers rely to a large extent on the researchers here to continue to develop techniques for improving UA. Today several students and a professor from the Agronomy Department are examining an experimental plot where some traditional crop varieties have been planted — varieties that have been shown to survive and thrive under less than ideal conditions, unlike some of the modern hybrids that require costly fertilizer. With them are workers from a local NGO and several CBOs that are participants in the project. Everyone is excited about the results. The plants are green and healthy despite being deliberately planted in poor soil. They have been supplemented with compost from one of the city's waste-recycling depots, and the impact is dramatic.

Moving on, we pay a brief visit to that recycling depot. This is one of six such depots strategically located throughout the urban area. In addition to the university, which consumes a large amount of the composted output, there is a large city park nearby, as well as a housing estate where space has also been designated as gardens for the residents. Each of the waste-recycling depots receives large amounts of organic waste matter, which is sorted and processed as required, then composted. The resulting product is sold by the bag or in bulk, depending on the quantities required. Residents of the housing estate drop by for one or two bags for their individual gardens. Students from the university bring a pick-up truck to take another load back to their experimental plots. Sales do not cover all the costs of maintaining these facilities, but they provide jobs, and the city has found that the reduction in the waste stream coupled with the effects of the compost in greening the urban area make the cost worthwhile.

Our next stop is at a large public park on the river. At first glance it looks much like any other well-kept city park — lots of green space and plenty of trees. But a closer examination shows that some of the green space is occupied by vegetable gardens, and some of the flower gardens are harvested daily to be sold. The trees provide shade, but many of them also provide fruit or nuts in season. Closer to the river is a low-lying area that typically floods every year. This is the dry season, however, and the flood plain is currently planted with a variety of nonfood crops, irrigated with water pumped by hand from the river. Groups of women and men are hard at work in several areas. They maintain the park without pay, in return for which they are allocated an area on which to plant their crops.

Organized groups of producers and processors like these are a key element of the city's strategy for incorporating UA into the mainstream of urban life. City managers and policymakers long ago recognized the importance of encouraging the city farmers to organize. This made it easier to resolve conflicts, to plan the most effective use of vacant space, and to involve them in the development of policies and regulations to fully integrate producers into the fabric of the city. Such groups enable farmers to work directly with NGOs and researchers to improve output, to keep abreast of what land is available for agriculture, to be involved in policy and planning exercises, and to join forces to process and market their produce.

We meet members of one such group at a low-cost housing development. Here the tenants' association allocates small plots of land to residents who want them (and most do). While some plant only what they need to supplement their family's diet, others cooperate to produce extra that can be sold at market. Some specialize in herbs and medicinal plants. All of them agree, however, that the gardens make a big difference in their lives. The children benefit from eating fresh produce daily, and the savings or the extra income is available for schoolbooks and other expenses. That there is land available for gardens here is thanks to the city planners, who collaborated in the design of the housing development with several organized producers' groups and community associations.

The gardens thrive in part because of the generous use of compost from the nearby recycling depot, but also because there is ample water for irrigation. When it built this high-density housing, the city incorporated an inexpensive greywater system that recycles water from hundreds of apartments. The water — from cooking, washing, and laundry — is filtered and then piped through a gravity-fed system to holding tanks that feed standpipes located at regular intervals throughout the garden areas. Using drip hoses and water cans, the residents are able to keep their gardens irrigated, even during the dry season, with water that otherwise would simply have poured into the city's already over-loaded sewer system.

We find a very different scene on the outskirts of the city. Here expansion has overrun what was until quite recently a small village, and the land that once supported subsistence farmers is now occupied by the large modern homes of wealthy citizens. In the past there were often angry confrontations, sometimes leading to violence, when villagers found themselves banished from lands that they had long considered their own. Intervention by city officials resulted in a compromise, however, which has allowed many of the villagers to continue to use some of the land. The city offered property tax reductions to the new owners as an incentive to allow controlled agricultural use of some of their lands at reasonable rents and on long-term leases. For their part, the farmers agreed to keep their livestock penned and to maintain the land appropriately. In this district the farmers have formed their own association, both to negotiate with the city and the landowners and to process and market their produce.

Heading back into the city we stop at a small food-processing plant. This business is run by a producers' cooperative representing several organized groups around the city. It is supported by the municipality, which assisted in transferring ownership of the abandoned building that now houses the plant and allows the cooperative a discount on property taxes. The plant currently employs only three people — all women — but sales to local supermarkets have been brisk, and there is talk of expansion. This would involve bringing other groups into the cooperative to increase supply, and negotiations are currently underway through a local NGO that has worked with the urban farmers for many years.

To market for our final stop. This is a street market in the centre of the city, one of a number that operate in different parts of the city on different days. The street is closed to traffic 2 days a week, and licensed vendors are displaying their wares in all their variety. Some have stalls, others set out their produce in baskets or boxes. There is a wide range of produce, from fresh greens, tomatoes, and beans, to eggplant, okra, and yams. Many of the stalls are operated by women, who represent one or more of the organized producer groups in the city. The atmosphere is friendly even as potential customers haggle over prices and comment on the quality of the produce. A city official monitors the proceedings and occasionally takes samples for testing to ensure that the produce meets health and quality standards.

Back to the present

Of course, all this is fiction. This is an imaginary city in an imagined future. No city in the world of today has all the pieces in place to support UA quite so coherently. But this vision of the future is by no means far-fetched. All of the parts described in our future city already exist. All of these things are happening today in different towns and cities as municipalities come to grips with the fact that, properly managed, UA is a huge potential benefit to urban life, not a nuisance to be eradicated.

In its ideal scenario for the city of the future, IDRC's CFP program listed a number of key principles:

→ **Integration into urban management** — supporting and valuing UA as an integral part of urban development and an effective tool for urban management;

→ **Self-reliant local food systems** — actively supporting UA through policies and research to develop a more robust urban food supply;

→ **Productive green spaces** — helping to purify the air and bridge the inequality of access to such spaces between rich and poor;

→ **Resource recovery** — recognizing the efficient treatment and reuse of solid and liquid wastes as a valuable resource for UA; and

➤ **Producer access** — organizing formerly marginalized producers into groups that can more effectively negotiate access, utilize research findings, and market their produce at a fair profit.

What is needed to build those cities of the future — better fed, healthier, wealthier, more equitable, and cleaner cities — is to build on the knowledge gained over the past 20 years. This knowledge can enhance the potential for UA to serve as a strategic tool to reduce urban food insecurity and poverty and to improve the urban environment.

IDRC and its partners have employed this knowledge to develop, package, and disseminate regionally tailored courses on the research and management of UA to teams of city governments, planners, managers, and NGOs (Smith et al. 2004; CIP 2005). There is a continuous demand for more and better training to reach new audiences of policymakers, researchers, and producers. This is slowly being met as the regional courses have given birth to manuals on concepts and methods, and trained graduates have succeeded in mainstreaming UA into the training curricula of their home institutions.

With a new generation of researchers and practitioners pressing the case for progress, the sustainable, healthier city of the future, with its productive green spaces within, on top of, and around its built environment, plus its prosperous market places, is surely only a short way down the road.

Glossary of Terms and Acronyms

AGROPOLIS: International Graduate Research Awards Program in Urban Agriculture (IDRC)

AGUILA: Red Latinoamericana de Investigaciones en Agricultura Urbana (Latin American Research Network on Urban Agriculture), Peru

Blackwater: Blackwater is wastewater from toilets and other disposal mechanisms of solid and liquid animal or human effluents (see *greywater*).

CBO: community-based organization

CEPIS: Centro Panamericano de Ingenieria Sanitaria y Ciencias Ambientales (Pan American Center for Sanitary Engineering and Environmental Sciences), Peru

CEUR/PUCMM: Centro de Estudios Urbanos y Regionales (Center for Urban and Regional Studies), Pontificia Universidad Catolica Madre y Maestra, Dominican Republic

CFP: Cities Feeding People program (IDRC)

CGIAR: Consultative Group on International Agriculture Research

CIDA: Canadian International Development Agency

CIP: Centro Internacional de la Papa (International Potato Center), Peru

DFID: Department for International Development, United Kingdom

DGIS: Directorate General of International Cooperation, Netherlands

Ecological footprint: The ecological footprint of a given population is "the total area of productive land and water required on a continuous basis to produce the resources consumed, and to assimilate the wastes produced, by that population, wherever on Earth the land (and water) is located" (Rees 1997).

ENDA: Environnement et développement du Tiers Monde (Environment and Development for the Third World), Senegal and Zimbabwe

EU: European Union

FAO: Food and Agriculture Organization of the United Nations

Food security: Food security means that food is available at all times; that all persons have means of access to it; that it is nutritionally adequate in terms of quantity, quality, and variety; and that it is acceptable within the given culture. Only when all these conditions are in place can a population be considered "food secure" (see Koc et al. 1999, pp. 1–7).

Foodshed: A restrictive definition would have the foodshed of a city correspond with the area next to a city whose food production is largely destined to supply the city in its daily food needs. A more encompassing definition has the foodshed of a city to include "all the areas that supply food products to it: local, rural, or foreign." The foodshed can be defined for each food group. Generally, the richer the city, the larger the foodshed (UNDP 1996, p. 10).

GIS: geographic information system

GMO: genetically modified organism

Greywater: Greywater is wastewater from washing, bathing, and laundry (see *blackwater*).

GTZ: Deutsche Gesellschaft für Technische Zusammenarbeit, Germany

IAGU: Institut africain de gestion urbaine (African Urban Management Institute), Senegal

IDRC: International Development Research Centre, Canada

IFAN: Institut fondamental d'Afrique noire (Basic Institute of Black Africa), Senegal

INWRDAM: Inter-Islamic Network on Water Resources and Development and Management, Jordan

IPES: Instituto Peruano de Promoción del Desarrollo Sostenible (Peruvian Institute for the Promotion of Sustainable Development)

IWMI: International Water Management Institute, Ghana and India

LAC: Latin America and the Caribbean

MDP-ESA: Municipal Development Partnership for Eastern and Southern Africa, Zimbabwe

NGO: nongovernmental organization

ONAS: Office national de l'assainissement du Sénégal (National Sanitation Agency), Senegal

PLAW: People, Land, and Water program (IDRC)

RUAF: International Network of Resource Centres on Urban Agriculture and Food Security, Netherlands

SDP: Sustainable Dar es Salaam Project, Tanzania

Self-reliance: A self-reliant community or city exploits to the fullest its own local resources, assets, and capacities to satisfy its own food needs, thereby reducing as much as possible its dependence on imports.

Self-sufficiency: Taking food supply for example, self-sufficiency refers to complete independence from imports to cater to a community or city's food needs, a goal hardly achievable even under the most optimistic scenario.

SENAR: Serviço Nacional de Aprendizagem Rural (National Rural Apprenticeship Service), Brazil

SGUA: Support Group on Urban Agriculture

Subsistence vs self-provisioning: Subsistence production was a term coined through research on peasant economies and rural societies largely isolated from market forces. In such economies, producers earmark most of their output for their own consumption. There is only minimal trade. In urban agriculture, the term has been applied to designate any portion of an urban producer's food output that they dispose of through nonmarket channels, including direct supplies to their own household. This usage has been criticized as inappropriate in urban settings, where a market economy prevails; here, food both produced and consumed at source does have monetary value (cost and benefit), and any effort to secure it at a lower cost than priced potentially brings cash savings. Instead, in urban agriculture, the term "self-provisioning" is increasingly used.

TOP: temporary occupancy permit

UA: Urban agriculture. There are many definitions of UA. CFP used the following: "An industry located within (intra-urban) or on the fringe (peri-urban) of a town, a city, or a metropolis, which grows or raises, processes, and distributes a diversity of food and nonfood products. It (re)uses on a daily basis human and natural resources, products, and services largely found in and around that urban area and, in turn, supplies on a daily basis human and material resources, products, and services largely to that urban area." **Intra-urban agriculture** refers to agriculture carried out within city limits (as defined by ratio of built-up area, population density, or administrative boundary line). **Peri-urban**

agriculture is carried out beyond that city limit and outward, up to a certain point. Where one sets the outer boundary of the peri-urban agricultural zone will depend on the criteria used, and several have been used in past research. But the degree of development of the local transportation infrastructure and system tends to be key in defining the "width" of this zone around the city (see *UPA*).

UMP: Urban Management Programme (UN-HABITAT), Ecuador and Kenya

UN: United Nations

UNCHS: United Nations Centre for Human Settlements, Kenya

UNDP: United Nations Development Programme

UN-HABITAT: United Nations Human Settlements Programme

UNICEF: United Nations Children's Fund

UPA: Urban and peri-urban agriculture, which includes both intra- and peri-urban agriculture (UPA and UA are used interchangeably in this book).

WHO: World Health Organization

WUF: World Urban Form

Appendix 2

Sources and Resources

The focus of this book is IDRC's support to research on urban agriculture. For those interested in learning more about the topic in general, there is a great deal of literature, both printed and on the Internet. This appendix of source material is organized into two sections. The first lists all those references specifically cited in this book. The second section lists Web sites and coordinates of selected IDRC research partners that were involved with the projects featured in this book. Note that for documents reporting on IDRC-funded research, the IDRC project number is listed at the end of the reference, like this: "(IDRC 101085)." This number can be used for further follow-up, such as when searching the main IDRC Web site, **www.idrc.ca**.

This book is an integral part of IDRC's thematic Web dossier on urban agriculture: **http://www.idrc.ca/in_focus_cities**. The full text of the book is available online and leads the reader into a virtual web of resources that explores two decades of research on UA. The Web site, which is duplicated on the CD that is packaged with this book, includes not only a thorough bibliography of UA research, but also a selection of case studies, full-text books, slide shows, and other useful resources.

References cited

Akinbamijo, Y.; Fall, S.T. 2002. Integrated peri-urban systems: horticulture and livestock in West Aftican cities. Final technical report. International Trypanotolerance Centre and Institut sénégalais de recherches agricoles, Banjul and Dakar, Senegal. (IDRC 003934)

Albuquerque, R. 1996a. Agricultura urbana para o saneamento e a geração de renda na região metropolitana de Fortaleza, Estado do Ceará, Brasil: estudo de viabilidade de hortas e arborização com frutíferas no Mutirão Serra Azul em Maracanaú.Grupo de Pesquisa e Intercambios Tecnológicos, Fortaleza, Brazil. (IDRC 003764)

———— 1996b. Estudo de viabilidade das lagoas de estabilização da Comunidade Habitacional Renascer Dias Macedo. Grupo de Pesquisa e Intercambios Tecnológicos, Fortaleza, Brazil. (IDRC 003764)

———— 1996c. Estudo de viabilidade para desenvolvimento da piscicultura na Comunidade de Amaní em Maranguapé. Grupo de Pesquisa e Intercambios Tecnológicos, Fortaleza, Brazil. (IDRC 003764)

———— 1999. Agricultura urbana, medio de generación de renta y transformación social: experiencias en la región metropolitana de Fortaleza, RMF. *In* FLACSO, IDRC, ed., Agricultura urbana en América Latina y el Caribe: impactos de proyectos de investigación. Cities Feeding People, IDRC, Ottawa, Canada. CFP Report No. 33, pp. 87–97. (IDRC 004514, IDRC 004542)

Bino, M.J.; Jayousi, O.; Al-Beiruti, S.N.; Jabay, O.; Sawan, J.; Al-Oran, A.; Burnat, J.; Laham, O. 2003. Fourth technical progress report. Inter-Islamic Network on Water Resources Development and Management, Amman, Jordan. (IDRC 100880)

Brundtland, G., ed. 1987. Our common future: report of the World Commission on Environment and Development. Oxford University Press, Oxford, UK. Available online at www.brundtlandnet.com/brundtlandreport.htm.

Cabannes, Y. 1997. Agriculture urbaine pour l'assainissement et la création de revenus dans l'agglomération de Fortaleza, Etat du Ceará, Brésil : rapport technique final. Grupo de Pesquisa e Intercambios Tecnológicos, Fortaleza, Brazil. (IDRC 003764)

Cabannes, Y.; Mougeot, L.J.A. 1999. El estado de la agricultura urbana en América latina y el Caribe. La Era Urbana, Suplemento para América latina y el Caribe, 1, iv–v. (IDRC 004155)

CEPIS (Centro Panamericano de Ingeniería Sanitaria y Ciencias Ambientales); PAHO (Pan American Health Organization); WHO (World Health Organization). 2002. Guidelines for the formulation of projects (a 15-step method for feasibility studies of municipal wastewater treatment projects designed to cater to a variety of agricultural uses). CEPIS, Lima, Peru. (IDRC 100123)

CIP (International Potato Centre). 1999. A CGIAR strategic initiative on urban and peri-urban agriculture: a proposal submitted for Finance Committee Strategic Research Funding. CIP, Lima, Peru. (IDRC 101085)

CIP (International Potato Centre); IDRC (International Development Research Centre). 2005. Urban agriculture: concepts and methods for research and management (interactive CD-ROM). Urban Harvest, CIP, Lima, Peru. (IDRC 101640)

Cissé, O.; Diop Gueye, N.F.; Sy, M. 2005. Institutional and legal aspects of urban agriculture in French-speaking West Africa: from marginalization to legitimization. Environment & Urbanization, 17(1), 143–154. (IDRC 100520)

COAG (Committee on Agriculture, FAO). 1999. Urban and peri-urban agriculture. Paper presented and approved at 15th Session of the COAG, 25–29 January 1999, FAO, Rome, Italy. COAG/99/10.

Collombon, J.-M.; Garcin, G.; Varlet, N. 1996. Valorização da produção de plantas aromáticas na região metropolitana de Fortaleza: estratégias para um desenvolvimento sustentável e propostas para um programa piloto em Pacatuba. Grupo de Pesquisa e Intercambios Tecnológicos , Fortaleza, Brazil. (IDRC 002748)

del Rosario, P.J.; Cornelio, Y.; Polanco, L.J.; Russell, A.; Lopez, H.; Escarraman, P. 1999. Manejo de residuos sólidos y agricultura urbana en la ciudad de Santiago de los Caballeros. Centro de Estudios Urbanos y Regionales, Pontifícia Universidad Católica Madre y Maestra, Santiago de los Caballeros, Dominican Republic. (IDRC 002759)

Dreschel, P.; Olufunke O.C.; Gyiele, L.; Amoah, P.; Danso, G.; Kamara A.; Forkuor, G. 2004. Improving the rural–urban nutrient cycle through urban and peri-urban agriculture: final narrative report (updated version). International Water Management Institute, Accra, Ghana. (IDRC 100376)

Egziabher, A.G.; Lee-Smith, D.; Maxwell, D.G.; Memon, P.A.; Mougeot, L.J.A.; Sawio, C.J. 1994. Cities feeding people: an examination of urban agriculture in East Africa. IDRC, Ottawa, Canada. Available online at www.idrc.ca/books.

Fall, S.T.; Fall, A.S., ed. 2001. Cités horticoles en sursis? L'agriculture urbaine dans les grandes Niayes au Sénégal. IDRC, Ottawa, Canada. Available online at www.idrc.ca/books. (IDRC 003934 and 100523)

Faruqui, N.I.; Niang, S.; Redwood, M. 2004. Untreated wastewater use in market gardens: a case study of Dakar, Senegal. In Scott, C.A.; Faruqui, N.I.; Raschid-Sally, L., ed., Wastewater use in irrigated agriculture: confronting the livelihood and environmental realities. CAB International, Cambridge, UK / IDRC, Ottawa, Canada / International Water Management Institute, Colombo, Sri Lanka. pp. 113–126. (IDRC 004367)

Hovorka, A. 1999. Women urban farmers: emerging trends and areas for future research. Paper presented at Women Farmers: Enhancing Rights and Productivity Conference, 26–27 August 1999, Centre for Development Research, Bonn, Germany.

IAGU (Institut africain de gestion urbaine). 2002. Consultation régionale des maires et autres acteurs africains de l'agriculture urbaine en Afrique francophone. IAGU, Dakar, Senegal. (IDRC 100520)

Kishimba, M.A. 1996. Urban agriculture in Dar es Salaam: how polluted are the irrigation waters? Chemistry Department, University of Dar es Salaam, Dar es Salaam, Tanzania. (IDRC 000219)

Koc, M.; MacRae, R.; Mougeot, L.J.A.; Welsh, J., ed. 1999. For hunger-proof cities: sustainable urban food systems. IDRC, Ottawa, Canada.

KUFSALC (Kampala Urban Food Security, Agriculture and Livestock Committee); UH (Urban Harvest). 2005. The Kampala City Urban Agriculture Ordinance: a guideline. KUFSALC, Kampala, Uganda. (IDRC 101085)

Kyessi, A. 1996. City expansion and urban agriculture in Dar es Salaam: lessons for planning. Centre for Human Settlements Studies, ARDHI Institute, Dar es Salaam, Tanzania. (IDRC 000219)

Lee-Smith, D.; Manundu, M.; Lamba, D.; Gathuru, P.K. 1987. Urban food production and the cooking fuel situation in urban Kenya. National report: results of a 1985 national survey. Mazingira Institute, Nairobi, Kenya. (IDRC 820114)

Maxwell, D.; Zziwa, S. 1992. Urban farming in Africa: The case of Kampala, Uganda. African Centre for Technology Studies Press, Nairobi, Kenya. (IDRC 880325)

MDP-ESA (Municipal Development Programme for Eastern and Southern Africa). 2001. The political economy of urban and peri-urban agriculture in Eastern and Southern Africa: proceedings of the MDP-ESA/IDRC workshop. MDP-ESA, Harare, Zimbabwe. (IDRC 100750)

———— 2002. Research project on accessing land for urban agriculture by the urban poor. Proceedings of a methodological workshop, 10–12 September, Kampala, Uganda. MDP-ESA, Harare, Zimbabwe. (IDRC 100519)

Mlozi, M.R.S.; Komba, A.; Geho, M.; Kimei, V. 2005. Improving urban poor's access to land for urban agriculture in Kinondoni Municipality, Tanzania. Sokoine University of Agriculture, Morogoro, Tanzania. (IDRC 100519)

Mougeot, L.J.A. 1994. The rise of city farming: research must catch up with reality. ILEIA Newsletter, 10(4), 4–5.

———— 1999. An improving domestic and international environment for African urban agriculture. African Urban Quarterly, 11(2–3), 137–153.

———— 2000. Urban agriculture: definition, presence, potentials and risks. In Bakker, N.; Dubbeling, M.; Gundel, S.; Sabel-Koschella, U.; de Zeeuw, H., ed., Growing cities, growing food: urban agriculture on the policy agenda. Cities Feeding People, IDRC, Ottawa, Canada. CFP Report No. 31. Available online at www.idrc.ca.

———— 2005. Introduction. In Mougeot, L.J.A., ed., AGROPOLIS: the social, political, and environmental dimensions of urban agriculture. Earthscan, London, UK / IDRC, Ottawa, Canada. pp. 1–29. Available online at www.idrc.ca/books.

Mubvami, T. 2004. Access to land for urban agriculture in Eastern and Southern africa: a synthesis report. Municipal Development Programme for Eastern and Southern Africa. Harare, Zimbabwe.

Mudimu, G.; Matinhure, N.; Mushayavanu, D.; Chingarande, S.; Toriro, P.; Muchopa, C. 2005. Research project on improving access to land for urban agriculture by the urban poor in Harare. University of Zimbabwe, Harare, Zimbabwe. (IDRC 100519)

Mushamba, S.; Mubvami, T.; Marongwe, N.; Chatiza, K., ed., 2003. Report on the Ministers' conference on urban and peri-urban agriculture in Eastern and Southern Africa: prospects for food security and growth (Harare Sheraton Conference Centre, Zimbabwe, 28-29 August 2003). Municipal Development Partnership for Eastern and Southern Africa, Harare, Zimbabwe. (IDRC 100519 and 003154)

Mwaiselage, A.A. 1996. Actors in urban agriculture in Dar es Salaam: potential and constraints. Centre for Human Settlements Studies, ARDHI Institute, Dar es Salaam, Tanzania. (IDRC 000219)

Nelson, T. 1996. Closing the nutrient loop. Worldwatch, 9(6), 10–17.

Niang, S. 1996. Utilisation des eaux usées domestiques en maraîchage périurbain à Dakar, Sénégal. Sécheresse, 7(3), 217–223. (IDRC 900153)

Niang, S.; Gaye, M., coord. 2002. L'épuration extensive des eaux usées pour la réutilisation dans l'agriculture urbaine: des technologies appropriées en zone sahelienne pour la lutte contre la pauvreté. Institut fondamental d'Afrique noire and ENDA Tiers-Monde/Relais pour le Développement Participatif, Dakar, Senegal. Rapport scientifique I. (IDRC 004367)

Nuwagaba, A.; Kyamanywa, C.; Kiguli, H.; Atukunda, G.; Mwesigwa, D. 2005. Improving urban poor's access to land for (peri)urban agriculture in Kampala City. Makerere University, Kampala, Uganda. (IDRC 100519)

PCC (Population Crisis Committee). 1990. Cities: life in the world's 100 largest metropolitan areas. PCC, Washington, DC, USA.

Premat, A. 2003. Small-scale urban agriculture in Havana and the re-production of the "new man" in contemporary Cuba. Revista Europea de Estudios Latinoamericanos y del Caribe, 75(October), 47–61. (IDRC 003754)

Prudencio, B.J., ed. 1997. Agricultura urbana en América latina. Memoria. Red Latino-americana de Investigaciones en Agricultura Urbana, Lima, Peru. (IDRC 002318)

PUCMM (Pontificia Universidad Catolica Madre y Maestra). 1998. Propuesta para la gestion de residuos sólidos en Santiago. PUCMM, Santiago de los Caballeros, Dominican Republic. (IDRC 002759)

Rees, W.E. 1997. Is "sustainable city" an oxymoron? Local Environment, 2(3), 303–308.

Régis, M.D.; Bartels, G.; Philoctete, G. 2000. Rapport final : projet horticulture urbaine. CARE Haïti, Pétionville, Haïti. (IDRC 119169)

Sachs, I. 1988. World food and energy in urban ecodevelopment. Economic and Political Weekly, 27 February 1988, 425–434.

Sawio, C. J. 1993. Feeding the urban masses? Towards an under-standing of the dynamics of urban agriculture and land-use change in Dar es Salaam, Tanzania. Graduate School of Geography, Clark University, Worcester, MA, USA. PhD dissertation. (IDRC 900123)

———— 1998. Managing urban agriculture in Dar es Salaam. Cities Feeding People, IDRC, Ottawa, Canada. CFP Report 20. (IDRC 000219)

Shakhatreh, H.; Raddad, K. 2000. Policies for urban agriculture in Jordan: a household survey in Amman. Department of Statistics, Hashemite Kingdom of Jordan, Amman, Jordan. (IDRC 003740)

Smith, O.B.; Moustier, P.; Mougeot, L.J.A.; Fall, A., ed., 2004. Développement durable de l'agriculture urbaine en Afrique francophone: enjeux, concepts et méthodes. Centre de coopération internationale en recherche agronomique pour le développement, Montpellier, France / IDRC, Ottawa, Canada. (IDRC 003754)

UMP-LAC (Urban Management Programme Latin America and the Caribbean, UN-HABITAT). 2001. Urban agriculture in cities of the 21st century: innovative approaches by local governments from Latin America and the Caribbean. UMP-LAC, Quito, Ecuador. Working Paper 84. (IDRC 004155)

UMP-LAC (Urban Management Programme Latin America and the Caribbean, UN-HABITAT); IPES (Peruvian Institute for the Promotion of Sustainable Development). 2003. Guidelines for municipal policymaking on urban agriculture. UMP-LAC, Quito, Ecuador. Available online at www.pgualc.org. (IDRC 100135-2)

UN (United Nations). 2004. World urbanization prospects: the 2003 revised population database. UN, New York, NY, USA. http://esa.un.org/unup/

UMP-LAC (Urban Management Programme Latin America and the Caribbean, UN-HABITAT); RUAF (Resource Centre on Urban Agriculture and Forestry). 2003. Optimising agricultural land use in the city area: access to land and water, adequate norms and regulations, integration in land use planning. Proceedings of the E-Conference, 3–22 November 2003. UMP-LAC, Quito, Ecuador / RUAF, Leusden, Netherlands. (IDRC 03154).

UNDP (United Nations Development Programme). 1996. Urban agriculture: food, jobs and sustainable cities. UNDP, New York, NY, USA.

UN-HABITAT (United Nations Human Settlements Programme). 2004. The state of the world's cities: globalization and urban culture. UN-HABITAT, Nairobi, Kenya.

World Bank. 1986. Poverty and hunger: issues and options for food security in developing countries. World Bank, Washington, DC, USA.

Research partners

Centro Internacional de Gestion Urbana
Av. Orellana E-938 y Yanez Pinzón, Edif. La Viña, 1er piso, Quito, Ecuador
Phone/fax: +593-2-250-6116
Email: cigu@cigu.org

Centro Panamericano de Ingenieria Sanitaria and Ciencias Ambientales
Los Pinos 259, Urb. Camacho La Molina, Lima 12, Peru
Phone: +51-1-437-1077
Fax: +51-1-437-8289
Email: cepis@cepis.ops-oms.org
Web: www.cepis.ops-oms.org

Chinese Academy of Sciences
52 Sanlihe Rd., Beijing 100864, China
Phone: +86-10-68597289
Fax: +86-10-68512458
Email: bulletin@mail.casipm.ac.cn
Web: english.cas.ac.cn/Eng2003/page/home.asp

Institut africain de gestion urbaine
BP 7263, Dakar, Senegal
Phone: +221-827-2200
Fax: +221-827-2813
Email: iagu@iagu.org
Web: www.iagu.org

Institut fondamental d'Afrique noire
Cheikh Anta Diop University, BP 206 UCAD Dakar, Senegal
Phone: +221-825-9890
Fax: +221-824-4918
Email: bifan@telecomplus.sn
Web: www.africainformation.net/ifan1.htm

Instituto Peruano de Promoción del Desarrollo Sostenible
Audiencia N1 194, San Isidro, Lima, Peru
Phone/fax: +51-1-440-6099, 421-9722, 421-6684
Email: ipes@ipes.org.pe
Web: www.ipes.org

Inter-Islamic Network on Water Resources Development and
Management
PO Box 1460, Jubeiha PC 11941 Amman, Jordan
Phone: +962-6-5332-993
Fax: +962-6-5332-969
Email: inwrdam@nic.net.jo
Web: www.inwrdam.org

International Network of Resource Centres on Urban Agriculture
and Food Security
PO Box 64, 3830 AB Leusden, Netherlands
Phone: +31-33-4326039
Fax: +31-33 4940791
Email: ruaf@etcnl.nl
Web: www.ruaf.org

International Water Management Institute
127, Sunil Mawatha, Pelawatte, Battaramulla, Sri Lanka
Phone: +94-11 2787404, 2784080
Fax: +94-11 2786854
Email: iwmi@cgiar.org
Web: www.iwmi.cgiar.org

International Water Management Institute (South Asia)
c/o ICRISAT, Patancheru, AP 502 324, India
Phone: +91-40-329-6161
Fax: 91-40-324-1239
Email: iwmi-india@cgiar.org
Web: www.iwmi.cgiar.org/southasia/index.asp

International Water Management Institute (Africa)
Private Bag X813, Silverton 0127, Pretoria, South Africa
Phone: +27-12-845-9100
Fax: +27-12-845-9110
Email: iwmi-africa@cgiar.org
Web: www.iwmi.cgiar.org/africa/index.asp

International Water Management Institute (Ghana)
PMB CT 112, Cantonments Accra, Ghana
Phone: +233-(0)21-784752-4
Fax: +233-(0)21-784752
Email: iwmi-ghana@cgiar.org
Web: www.iwmi.cgiar.org/africa/west_africa/index.htm

Kinondoni Municipal Council
PO Box 31902, Dar es Salaam, Tanzania
Phone: +255-22-2170173
Fax: +255-22-2172951
Email: kinondoni@costech.or.tz
Web: www.kinondonimunicipality.go.tz

The Mazingira Institute
PO Box 14550, 00800 Nairobi, Kenya
Phone: +254-020-4443219/26/29
Fax: +254-020-4444643
Email: mazinst@mitsuminet.com
Web: www.mazinst.org

Municipal Development Partnership
Eastern and Southern Africa Regional Office
7th Floor Hurudza House, 14-16 Nelson Mandela Avenue,
Harare, Zimbabwe
Phone: +263-4-774385/6, 724356-7
Fax: +263-4-774387
Email: gmatovu@mdpafrica.org.zw
Web: www.mdpafrica.org

Urban Harvest
c/o CIP (Convening Center), PO Box 1558, Lima 12, Peru
Tel: +51-1-317-5346
Fax: +51-1-317-5326
Email: urbanharvest@cgiar.org
Web: www.cipotato.org/urbanharvest

United Nations Human Settlements Programme (UN-HABITAT)
PO Box 30030, Nairobi, Kenya
Phone: +254-20-623120
Fax: +254-20-623477
Email: infohabitat@unhabitat.org
Web: www.unhabitat.org

The Publisher

The International Development Research Centre is a public corporation created by the Parliament of Canada in 1970 to help researchers and communities in the developing world find solutions to their social, economic, and environmental problems. Support is directed toward developing an indigenous research capacity to sustain policies and technologies developing countries need to build healthier, more equitable, and more prosperous societies.

IDRC Books publishes research results and scholarly studies on global and regional issues related to sustainable and equitable development. As a specialist in development literature, IDRC Books contributes to the body of knowledge on these issues to further the cause of global understanding and equity. The full catalogue is available at **www.idrc.ca/books.**